Is Democracy Fair?

The Mathematics of Voting and Apportionment

Leslie Johnson Nielsen and Michael de Villiers

KEY CURRICULUM PRESS

Innovators in Mathematics Education

Authors: **Leslie Johnson Nielsen** and **Michael de Villiers**

Editor: Crystal Mills

Editorial Assistant: Jeff Gammon

Reviewers: Albert Goetz, Phillip Straffin

Researcher: Ron Heckart

Illustrations: Ryan Alexiev

Cover Design: Christy Butterfield

Interior Design
and Production: Kristen Garneau

Key Curriculum Press
1150 65th Street
Emeryville, CA 94608
510-595-7000
editorial@keypress.com
http://www.keypress.com

10 9 8 7 6 5 4 3   05   04   03   02
ISBN 1-55953-277-7
Printed in the United States of America

TABLE OF CONTENTS

• PREFACE

School mathematics is often taught almost completely divorced from real-world contexts and from other subjects in the curriculum. This is particularly unfortunate because mathematics today is increasingly applied to more and more problems that affect our daily lives, from solving problems of traffic congestion to combating pollution, from preserving natural resources like water and soil to effectively managing a business, from finding a cure for AIDS to developing improved satellite communications.

The original draft of this book was motivated by the first fully democratic elections in South Africa in April 1994. It was a time of great excitement and anticipation as everyone looked forward to finally closing the sad chapter of apartheid in South Africa's history. It was also a time of heated debate among South Africa's politicians, political scientists, and public regarding the best system of voting and representation for the new South Africa. The ideal of representative democracy—one-person, one-vote—is a simple idea, but to achieve this ideal in practice is not. How is a fair and just system ensured? What criteria can be used to evaluate and compare different systems?

One of the intentions of the original book was to not only bring various options to the attention of the different political parties at South Africa's negotiating forum, but to also discuss in a fairly nontechnical manner some of the mathematical pros and cons of each method. Although copies of the original book were sent to representatives of each of the major parties, it is not clear whether it had any influence on the finally adopted Interim Constitution. (In fact, Hamilton's method was chosen as the apportionment method for the historic elections in April 1994, despite the book—and an article of mine in the influential *Finance Week*—pointing out its vulnerability to the Alabama paradox.) However, it is perhaps noteworthy that although proportional representation has been accepted in South Africa's final constitution, adopted in May 1996, no specific method of apportionment is prescribed.

A more important intention of the original draft was to emphasize the following educational objectives, which are also appropriate for this new, expanded book:

- To demonstrate to students the applicability of mathematics to the analysis of problems in the seemingly nonmathematical context of the social and political sciences;

- To challenge the stereotype that mathematics is of value only in certain applied sciences like physics, chemistry, and computer science;

- To contribute to voter education in general by exposing students to several different alternatives together with a discussion of the strengths and weaknesses of those alternatives.

I hereby wish to thank Crystal Mills and Leslie Nielsen for their excellent work in substantially editing, expanding, and refining the original book to its present form. The new version provides an excellent opportunity for a multidisciplinary approach by teachers from diverse subject areas.

Michael de Villiers
University of Durban-Westville, South Africa
May 1996

NOTE TO THE TEACHER

One of the interesting challenges of teaching is finding ways to connect two different subject areas so that both subjects are interesting and accessible. Often when we connect mathematics to the social sciences, it is only to calculate statistics and graph results. In this book of activities, the mathematics is interesting yet not overly difficult. The social studies/political science aspect of the activities is fascinating.

This book can be used in any number of ways. You can do an activity once a week, or you can do an intense unit on the mathematics of voting. You can do the activities in a social studies class or in a mathematics class, or you can team teach. You can choose to do the activities on voting, the activities on apportionment, or both.

The book is divided into two sections. The first eight activities cover voting methods and election decision procedures. They are devoted to the question of how a group can fairly elect one or more candidates from a field of three or more.

In the second section, students explore the topic of apportionment. Activity 9 is a general introduction to the problem of apportionment. In Activities 10 through 17, students explore methods of apportionment that have been considered for apportioning representatives to the U.S. House of Representatives. In Activity 18, students are introduced to proportional representation, in which representatives are apportioned by party rather than by geographical location.

Each activity contains a section called **Consider This**. Students should work on this part of the activity in groups. This section of the activity will introduce them to new ideas and ask them to discuss and evaluate methods. At times they will actually apply an election decision procedure or apportionment method. Encourage students to take notes on their procedures and results for use in later activities. After students have completed a Consider This section, you should have the class regroup to discuss the results of the group work. In some cases, each group will represent a constituency, and, as a result, an interesting debate may take place.

In the sections called **Explore Further**, students continue exploring an election decision procedure or an apportionment method. The questions in these sections are designed to be appropriate for homework, although they can also be assigned as group work to be done in the classroom. In these sections, students will often uncover flaws and problems in the methods they are exploring.

Many of the activities contain a section labeled **Research**. In these sections, students are asked to research historical background as well as current political situations. Much of the information can be found in encyclopedias and almanacs or in other library sources. If your students have access to the Internet, they will find much useful information there. It is helpful to discuss with them keywords they can use in their search. You may need to clarify how thoroughly you want your students to research a topic.

The sections labeled **Calculator Exploration** are optional. Encourage your students to use calculators whenever they think they will be helpful. With the aid of programmable calculators or computer spreadsheet programs, students will be able to explore some of the apportionment methods in much more detail and will be able to concentrate on the results of the methods rather than the calculations involved. Some of your students may want to write their own programs. Calculator programs for most of the apportionment methods follow Activity 18. You can duplicate the blackline master, or, after inputting the programs into one calculator, students can use their linking cables to transfer the programs.

The **Research Project** is meant to be a long-term project to accompany activities in the second part of the book. This project can be assigned anytime after students have completed Activity 9. However, be sure to discuss the idea of proportional representation, which is presented in Activity 18, before students start their research. You can decide how to assign students to countries. One model is to ask students to draw names of countries out of a hat. You could make this a group project and have each group be responsible for reporting on a country. You might want to assign several countries to each student or group in the event that some embassies do not respond to requests for information. You can find addresses for embassies in some almanacs. The following internet address has a lot of information on electoral systems as well as recent election results (or at least it did when the book went to press): http://www/keele.ac.uk/depts/po/election.htm1.

LIST OF COUNTRIES

Countries that use plurality or "winner take all" voting methods

Antigua/Bahamas	India
Barbados	Jamaica
Canada	St. Christopher
France	St. Lucia
Great Britain	St. Vincent
Grenada	Trinidad and Tobago
Haiti	United States of America

Countries that use some form of proportional representation

Angola	Greece	New Zealand
Argentina	Guyana	Nicaragua
Australia	Hungary	Norway
Austria	Iceland	Panama
Bangladesh	Ireland	Peru
Belgium	Israel	Poland
Bolivia	Italy	Portugal
Brazil	Japan	Senegal
Chile	Liechtenstein	South Africa
Columbia	Luxembourg	Spain
Costa Rica	Madagascar	Sweden
Denmark	Malta	Switzerland
Dominican Republic	Mexico	Surinam
El Salvador	Mozambique	Uruguay
Finland	Nauru	Venezuela
Germany	Netherlands	

RESEARCH PROJECT

In the activities in *Is Democracy Fair?* you will be exploring voting and apportionment methods. In the process, you will encounter references to countries that use some of the methods presented. As you proceed through the activities, you will also be doing a long-term research project on a government other than that of the United States. You will present the results of your research project to your class in a form that your teacher will specify.

The following questions can help guide your research:

- How are the citizens in the country you chose represented in their government?

- Does this country have an elected president or prime minister (or both)?

- How many candidates usually run for this position in an election?

- What type of ballot is used in elections?

- What election decision procedure is used?

- Does this country have a representative body like the U.S. Congress?

- How are the representatives elected?

- Are people represented geographically or by party?

- How many parties does the country have?

- How are representatives apportioned to this congress? What apportionment method is used?

- If you can get the results of a recent election, include them in your report.

Use the following questions to help you analyze the information you collect:

- Why do you think the people in your country chose the voting and apportionment methods they did?

- What strengths do the methods they chose have?

- What problems, if any, do you notice as a result of the methods your country uses?

Following are some suggested sources of information:

- Start at your library. Find out as much as you can about the country. Try encyclopedias and almanacs.

- Search on the Internet to see what information you can gather about the country you have chosen.

- Write letters to your country's embassy. You may be given another address, perhaps in the country itself, to write to. International mail takes about a week-to-ten-days in each direction, so be sure to send your letters early!

PLURALITY ELECTION DECISION PROCEDURE

Your math class has just won the grand prize in the math-a-thon fund-raiser—a free pizza lunch! The pizza parlor is offering a special deal if you order only one type of pizza. The choices are ham and pineapple pizza, pepperoni and mushroom pizza, and veggie delight pizza. Hold an election in your class now. Each person can vote for one pizza.

Consider This . . .

1. Work with your group to analyze the results of the election. Enter the number of votes each pizza candidate receives in the table below. Then compute the percentage of the total votes that each pizza received.

Type of pizza	Number of votes	Percentage of votes
Ham and pineapple		
Pepperoni and mushroom		
Veggie delight		

- Which pizza won?

- Did your pizza win?

- Are you satisfied with the results of the election? Why or why not?

• Do you feel that the election was fair? Explain.

The method you used to choose a pizza is called the **plurality election decision procedure**. It is
the way in which many countries hold elections, and chances are it is how you vote for a student
council representative and make other important decisions in your school. When you hold an election
this way, you use a **standard ballot** on which you vote only for your first choice. Does this method
of election ensure the selection of the *choice of the people?*

2. The class that won the geography-a-thon also won a pizza lunch, and the results of their
   vote are displayed in the table below. Compute the percentage of votes for each type of
   pizza and enter these percentages in the table.

Type of pizza	Number of votes	Percentage of votes
Ham and pineapple	12	
Pepperoni and mushroom	8	
Veggie delight	13	

• Do you think the class was satisfied with the results of this election? Why or why
  not?

• What do you think would have been the result if the choice of pizzas had been
  between a veggie pizza and a meat pizza?

In any election in which there are more than two candidates, it is possible for the least popular
candidate to win. This happens when the majority of votes are split between two or more similar
choices. It can occur in choosing pizzas, in student council elections, and in political elections.

Explore Further

3. In an election with 1000 voters in which the plurality method is used, what is the
   smallest percentage of the total vote by which a candidate could be elected if there are
   three candidates? Four candidates? Five candidates? Ten candidates? n candidates?

4. How fair do you think the plurality method is in cases with more than two candidates?
   Does the plurality method become more or less fair as the number of candidates increases?

5. The plurality method is still widely used in many countries, such as Great Britain and
   countries historically influenced by Great Britain, including the United States, New
   Zealand, Canada, and India. Now that you have explored the plurality method of election,
   do you think that it is a fair method? Was it a fair way for your class to choose its pizza?
   Is it a fair way to choose an elected official?

6. Describe a situation in which you were asked to make a choice or to vote using the
   plurality method. Do you think the results were fair? Why or why not?

Calculator Exploration

7. The integer function, INT(x), is very useful in creating formulas to model situations in which you want the answer to be a whole number. It is defined so that INT(x) of any real number x is the largest integer smaller than or equal to x; for example, INT(3.7) = 3. Your calculator may have an INT function built in. See if you can find it, and use it to find each value below.

    a. INT(4.2)   b. INT(1.99)

    c. INT(0.24)   d. INT(12.01)

    e. INT(–4.21)   f. INT(0.15)

8. Graph each of the functions below. Be sure your calculator is set to dot mode rather than connected mode. Write a description of each function based on the graph. Use the trace function to help you interpret the graph.

    a. $y = \text{INT}(x)$ b. $y = -\text{INT}(x)$ c. $y = -\text{INT}(-x)$

9. Consider an election with m voters and n candidates. Write a formula using the INT function that will allow you to find the smallest percentage of the total vote by which a candidate could be elected using the plurality method.

Research

10. In the United States, there are traditionally two candidates for president. In some presidential elections, however, there has been a third candidate. Do some research and find out in how many presidential elections there has been a third candidate. How many of these candidates do you think had a significant impact on the outcome of the election?

TEACHER'S NOTES

This is an introductory activity that explores the most common method of voting in the United States. Voters are usually asked to choose one candidate from a slate of two or more. The votes are counted, and whoever receives the most votes wins. This process of choosing a winner is called the **plurality election decision procedure.**

Students discover in this activity that the plurality method has a weakness. In elections with more than two candidates, a candidate can win without obtaining a majority of the votes cast. In an election among three candidates, if two of them have similar views, they may split the votes, allowing a candidate who might be the least popular to win. This situation is presented in the example of the hypothetical class that won the geography-a-thon. The two different kinds of meat pizzas split the majority of the votes so that the veggie delight pizza won. If the students who preferred a meat pizza had agreed on one type of meat pizza before the vote was taken, the result would have been different.

In Question 1, students are asked to analyze the results of the class's pizza election. After they have analyzed the results, encourage a class discussion. In Question 2, students are asked to discuss their impressions of the election described in the activity. After the groups have had time to discuss the questions, ask them to report back to the class as a whole. Students may be surprised at the weakness inherent in the plurality method. Encourage them to discuss this weakness, as well as possible solutions to the problem of elections with multiple candidates.

Answers

Consider This . . .

1. Answers may vary.

2.

Type of pizza	Percentage of votes
Ham and pineapple	36.36
Pepperoni and mushroom	24.24
Veggie delight	39.39

Answers may vary. Perhaps those students who prefer ham and pineapple pizza would have voted with the students preferring pepperoni and mushroom pizza, and a meat pizza would have won.

Explore Further

3.

Number of candidates	Percentage of votes needed to win
3	>33.$\overline{3}$
4	>25
5	>20
10	>10
n	>$\frac{100}{n}$

4. The plurality method becomes unfair as soon as there is more than one candidate. As the number of candidates increases, the possibility of a very unpopular candidate winning also increases.

5. Answers may vary.

6. Answers may vary.

Calculator Exploration

7. a. **4**   b. **1**   c. **0**   d. **12**   e. **−5**   f. **0**

8. a. The function returns the largest integer smaller than or equal to x.

   b. The function returns the opposite of the largest integer smaller than or equal to x.

   c. The function returns the smallest integer greater than or equal to x.

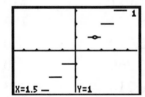

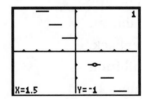

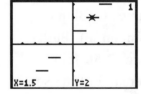

9. $$\frac{100\left[\text{INT}\left(\dfrac{m}{n}\right)+1\right]}{m}$$

Research Question

10. Answers will vary.

Presidential election results in years in which there were more than two candidates:

Year	Candidate	Party	Popular vote	Electoral vote
1796	John Adams	Federalist		71
	Thomas Jefferson	Dem-Rep		68
	Thomas Pickney	Federalist		59
	Aaron Burr	Dem-Rep		30
	Scattering			48
1800	Thomas Jefferson	Dem-Rep		73
	Aaron Burr	Dem-Rep		73
	John Adams	Federalist		65
	Charles C. Pinckney	Federalist		64
	John Jay	Federalist		1
1876	Rutherford B. Hayes	Republican	4,033,768	185
	Samuel J. Tilden	Democratic	4,285,992	184
	Peter Cooper	Greenback	81,737	0
1880	James A. Garfield	Republican	4,449,053	214
	Winfield S. Hancock	Democratic	4,442,035	155
	James B. Weaver	Greenback	308,578	0
1884	Grover Cleveland	Democratic	4,911,017	219
	James G. Blaine	Republican	4,848,334	182
	Benjamin F. Butler	Greenback	175,379	0
	John P. St. John	Prohibition	150,369	0
1888	Benjamin Harrison	Republican	5,440,216	233
	Grover Cleveland	Democratic	5,538,233	168
	Clinton B. Fisk	Prohibition	249,506	0
	Alson J. Streeter	Union Labor	146,935	0
1892	Grover Cleveland	Democratic	5,556,918	277
	Benjamin Harrison	Republican	5,176,108	145
	James B. Weaver	People's	1,041,028	22
	John Bidwell	Prohibition	264,133	0
1912	Woodrow Wilson	Democratic	6,286,214	435
	Theodore Roosevelt	Progressive	4,126,020	88
	William H. Taft	Republican	3,483,922	8
	Eugene V. Debs	Socialist	897,011	0
1968	Richard M. Nixon	Republican	31,785,480	301

	Hubert Humphrey	Democratic	31,275,166	191
	George C. Wallace	American Independent	9,906,473	46
1992	William J. Clinton	Democratic	44,909,889	370
	George H. Bush	Republican	39,104,545	168
	H. Ross Perot	Independent	19,742,267	0

ORDINAL AND CARDINAL BALLOTS

In Activity 1, you discovered that the plurality method of voting does not always give fair results. In this and subsequent activities, you will investigate other methods of making election decisions. You need to consider two aspects of an election: the type of ballot and what to do with the information once the ballots have been completed.

First, you will investigate different types of ballots. For the voter, changing the ballot is the most dramatic and obvious way to change the election procedure.

Changing the ballot is the most obvious way to change the election decision procedure.

Ordinal Ballots

One type of ballot that can be used is called an **ordinal ballot**. To create an ordinal ballot, you ask the voters to rank their preferences. Voters can either list their preferences in order from most to least favorite or assign a number to each candidate in order of preference. The finished list ranking each voter's preferences is called a **preference schedule.**

Rank your pizza choice. Put 1 by your first choice, 2 by your second choice, and 3 by your last choice.

Choice	Rank
Ham and pineapple	
Pepperoni and mushroom	
Veggie delight	

If a student likes pepperoni and mushroom pizza best but prefers ham and pineapple pizza to veggie delight pizza, she would mark her ballot like the one below.

Rank your pizza choice. Put 1 by your first choice,
2 by your second choice, and 3 by your last choice.

Choice	Rank
Ham and pineapple	2
Pepperoni and mushroom	1
Veggie delight	3

Her preference schedule
would look like this:

Pepperoni and mushroom
Ham and pineapple
Veggie delight

Consider This . . .

1. Katrine likes veggie delight pizza best and is indifferent between the other two pizzas, which means that she likes them equally well. How would she mark her ballot?

2. Schuyler likes veggie delight pizza best, thinks pepperoni and mushroom pizza would be okay, and really dislikes ham and pineapple pizza. How would he mark his ballot?

3. If Katrine and Schuyler had used a standard ballot in which they voted only for their favorite, their votes would have been the same. What information would have been lost? How important is this information?

4. Use ordinal ballots to take a vote in your math class among the three types of pizza. Once everyone has voted, tally the votes and summarize the results using preference schedules.

   • How will you decide which pizza is the winner? Discuss with your group how you think the winner should be determined and then share your decision with the class.

   • Did all groups come to the same conclusion? If not, can you imagine situations in which different class members might disagree about how the winner should be determined?

Cardinal Ballots

If you want to get even more information from your voters, you can use a cardinal ballot. In a cardinal ballot, you ask voters to rank their choices on a predetermined scale. This type of ballot might tell you more specifically that a student prefers pepperoni and mushroom pizza only a little bit more than ham and pineapple pizza but prefers ham and pineapple pizza much more than veggie delight pizza.

Rank each pizza choice on a scale of 1 to 10,
where 10 is the highest score.

Choice	Rank
Ham and pineapple	
Pepperoni and mushroom	
Veggie delight	

5. Fill out the cardinal ballot for pizza with your own preferences and discuss the following questions with the other students in your group.

   • What information does your completed cardinal ballot give that the standard and ordinal ballots don't?

   • Which type of ballot do you prefer?

   • Which type of ballot would you want to use to vote for something important to you?

Explore Further

6. If the voters in your class can always rank the pizzas from most to least favorite, then we can say that they are never indifferent among the pizza choices. If voters can't be indifferent, how many preference schedules are possible using ordinal ballots if there are four different pizza types? Five pizza types? n pizza types?

7. In another class, some of the students are indifferent about the pizza choices. List the different preference schedules that are possible using ordinal ballots in their vote between the three different types of pizza. How many different preference schedules are possible?

8. With four pizza types, there are 75 different preference schedules. Make a statement about what happens as the number of choices gets larger and students are indifferent.

9. Ordinal ballots are used extensively in Australia and to a lesser degree in the Republic of Ireland and Malta. Ordinal and cardinal ballots are often used also in consumer or other surveys.

   • Give some examples of times when you have been asked to fill in a cardinal or ordinal ballot.

   • Did you feel that you were able to represent your views accurately?

   • Comment on some possible advantages and disadvantages of using ordinal and cardinal ballots.

10. The geology class has scheduled a field trip, and the students have to agree where to go. The choices are Grand Canyon, Bryce Canyon, or Death Valley. They take a vote using ordinal ballots. The results are displayed in the table below.

Number of students with this preference schedule	7	4	8	6	5
	Grand Canyon	Bryce Canyon	Death Valley	Death Valley	Grand Canyon
	Bryce Canyon	Grand Canyon	Bryce Canyon	Grand Canyon	Death Valley
	Death Valley	Death Valley	Grand Canyon	Bryce Canyon	Bryce Canyon

Several of the students argue that, based on the vote, the class should go to Death Valley. The rest of the class disagrees. After a heated debate, some of the students say that Death Valley is the winner using the plurality method. Do you agree with them? How do you use preference schedules to determine a winner based on the plurality method? How would you suggest the class make a fair decision based on the preference schedules?

Calculator Exploration

11. Use your calculator to calculate $n!$, n^2, and 2^n for the values of n in the table below.

n	$n!$	n^2	2^n
1			
2			
3			
4			
5			
6			
7			
8			
9			
10			

12. Look at your results in Question 11. Experiment with your calculator to see if the same relationship holds for large values of n.

13. Based on your answers to Questions 11 and 12, describe some of the difficulties with ordinal ballots.

Research

14. Design an ordinal ballot for a survey on a topic of your choice. Collect responses from 20 or more people. Summarize the results of your survey. Save the ballots you collect for use in a later activity.

TEACHER'S NOTES

In this activity, students are introduced to alternatives to the standard ballot, on which voters mark only their first choice. Both ordinal ballots and cardinal ballots enable voters to give more information regarding their preferences.

In the formation of new voting procedures in South Africa, arguments against the use of ordinal ballots were based on the high levels of illiteracy and innumeracy. Illiteracy and innumeracy are growing problems in the United States, so the same argument could possibly be applied here as well. It might be interesting to hold a class discussion on whether students believe voters are capable of using ordinal and cardinal ballots successfully.

In the Consider This section, students are asked to consider how a voter should mark a ballot if he or she is indifferent between candidates. In general, if a voter is indifferent between candidates, he or she assigns them the same number. A blackline master of pizza ballots is at the end *of this* activity.

Be sure to save the results of the pizza vote for use in future activities.

Questions 6, 7, and 8 introduce some basic combinatoric principles. Question 6 can be used to introduce the concept of factorial. As your students approach these problems, encourage them to use problem-solving techniques such as looking at simpler cases, drawing a sketch or table, and looking for a pattern.

Conclude this activity with a discussion of how students would like to process the data from their pizza vote. This discussion leads directly into the next activity, which begins a series of activities on election decision procedures. If the students' vote gives a clear-cut winner, you might want to provide some simulated results that lead to a more interesting discussion, such as the data from Question 9 in Explore Further.

The Research question asks students to design their own survey and collect "ballots" from at least 20 people. These results can also be used in the research sections of Activities 3–8. You might have students work with their groups to design questions that will elicit good results. Students will enjoy analyzing results using their own collected data.

Answers

Consider This . . .

1. Katrine would put 1 by the veggie delight and 2 by the other two types of pizza.

2. Schuyler would put 1 by the veggie delight pizza, 2 by the pepperoni and mushroom pizza, and 3 by the ham and pineapple pizza.

3. The information lost is that if Katrine couldn't have veggie pizza, she would be equally happy with the other two, but Schuyler would not be happy with the ham and pineapple pizza.

4. Answers will vary. This question provides an excellent opportunity for students to discuss and compare their conclusions.

5. The cardinal ballot allows the voter to express how strong his preferences are. Other answers will vary.

Explore Further

6. For 4 pizza types, there are 24 possible preference schedules. For 5 pizza types, there are 120 possible preference schedules, and for n pizza types, there are n! different possible preference schedules. Encourage students to make a table to solve this problem.

Number of pizza types	1	2	3	4	5	...	n
Number of preference schedules	1	2	6	24	120	...	n!

7. Let H, P, and V stand for the three types of pizza. If there are three types of pizza, there are 13 different possible preference schedules.

HPV	H P V	H V P	H PV	P H V	P V H	P HV	V P H	V H P	V PH	VP H	HV P	HP V

8. As the number of candidates increases, the number of different preference schedules increases dramatically.

9. Answers will vary.

10. Using the plurality method, Death Valley is the winner with 14 votes. Grand Canyon has 12 votes, and Bryce Canyon has 4 votes. Answers will vary for the second question.

Calculator Exploration

11.

n	n!	n²	2ⁿ
1	1	1	1
2	2	4	4
3	6	9	8
4	24	16	16
5	120	25	32
6	720	36	64
7	5,040	49	128
8	40,320	64	256
9	362,880	81	512
10	3,628,800	100	1,024

12. For $n > 4$, $n!$ has the largest value.

13. Some people may argue that ordinal ballots can be too complicated for some voters. However, it can also be argued that many people can keep track of complex scoring systems in games, and can rank their favorite players by statistics. It would seem that these same people could use a complicated system to voice their preferences. People may also have difficulty analyzing or understanding the results because of the number of preference schedules that may result depending on the number of choices and on whether or not voters express indifference.

Research

14. Answers will vary.

Pizza Ballots

Rank your pizza choice. Put 1 by your first choice, 2 by your second choice, and 3 by your last choice.

Choice	Rank
Ham and pineapple	
Pepperoni and mushroom	
Veggie delight	

Rank your pizza choice. Put 1 by your first choice, 2 by your second choice, and 3 by your last choice.

Choice	Rank
Ham and pineapple	
Pepperoni and mushroom	
Veggie delight	

Rank your pizza choice. Put 1 by your first choice, 2 by your second choice, and 3 by your last choice.

Choice	Rank
Ham and pineapple	
Pepperoni and mushroom	
Veggie delight	

Rank your pizza choice. Put 1 by your first choice, 2 by your second choice, and 3 by your last choice.

Choice	Rank
Ham and pineapple	
Pepperoni and mushroom	
Veggie delight	

Rank your pizza choice. Put 1 by your first choice, 2 by your second choice, and 3 by your last choice.

Choice	Rank
Ham and pineapple	
Pepperoni and mushroom	
Veggie delight	

Rank your pizza choice. Put 1 by your first choice, 2 by your second choice, and 3 by your last choice.

Choice	Rank
Ham and pineapple	
Pepperoni and mushroom	
Veggie delight	

RUN-OFF ELECTIONS

When a country or organization decides to hold elections, it not only has to choose what type of ballot to use, but it also has to decide how to use the information from the ballots to choose a winner. This process of choosing a winner is called the **election decision.** When a group uses a standard ballot to hold an election, the plurality election decision procedure is used to determine the winner. If there is no clear winner, then a revote must take place in which the voters have to return to the polls. If the group uses ordinal or cardinal ballots and no candidate obtains a majority vote, it isn't necessary for the voters to return to the polls. The information from their ballots about their preferences can be used to determine a winner using a run-off election decision procedure.

The sequential pairwise method is used in the U.S. House of Representatives when voting on legislation.

In Activity 2, you examined ordinal and cardinal ballots and voted using ordinal ballots. You may have had a heated discussion about how to use the information from your vote fairly. Were you able to agree on a method for deciding the winner? In this activity, you will explore several election decision procedures that students in a physics class used in trying to make their pizza decision.

The physics class at Central City High earned a pizza party for having designed and built a new, effortless teeter-totter for the local playground. They had to choose one of four types of pizza, and they wanted to be sure that everyone in their class thought the choice was fair. They decided to use ordinal ballots. After voting, they put the results on the board using preference schedules, listing the favorite pizza on each schedule first. The results are summarized in the table below.

Number of students with this preference schedule	8	5	6	7
	Pepperoni	Ham	Veggie	Sausage
	Ham	Veggie	Ham	Ham
	Veggie	Sausage	Sausage	Veggie
	Sausage	Pepperoni	Pepperoni	Pepperoni

Standard Run-Off Election

Although pepperoni pizza got more first-place votes than any other pizza, it did not get a majority. To determine the winner, the class chooses to have a run-off election. Because they used ordinal ballots, they do not need to vote again. All the information they need can be extracted from the preference schedules. To hold the run-off election, the class eliminates all the candidates except the top two, that is the two pizzas that got the most first-place votes. So the run-off election will be between pepperoni pizza and sausage pizza. To determine the new preference schedules, remove veggie pizza and ham pizza, and move up pepperoni pizza and sausage pizza to fill in the blank spaces.

Number of students with this preference schedule	8	5	6	7
	Pepperoni	Sausage	Sausage	Sausage
	Sausage	Pepperoni	Pepperoni	Pepperoni

In this run-off, pepperoni gets 8 first-place votes and sausage gets 18.

Consider This . . .

1. In your group, use the run-off procedure to select a winner from the election your class held in Activity 2.

2. How does the run-off procedure compare to the plurality method? Use the following questions to help guide your discussion.

    •   Do you think this method is more fair than the plurality method?
        Why or why not?

    •   Do you think more students would be satisfied with the results? Why or why not?

    •   Would fewer students be really unhappy? Why or why not?

Hare Elimination

There are several variations of the run-off procedure. One variation is the **Hare elimination**, sometimes called a **sequential run-off**. To use this method, refer to the ballots and repeatedly eliminate the least favorite choice until a single victor emerges. This method differs from the standard run-off procedure in that you create new preference schedules each time a choice is eliminated. The physics class decided to experiment with a sequential run-off. By looking at the preference schedule on the board, they could see that ham pizza had the fewest first-place votes, so they removed it and got the following preference schedule.

Number of students with this preference schedule	8	5	6	7
	Pepperoni	Veggie	Veggie	Sausage
	Veggie	Sausage	Sausage	Veggie
	Sausage	Pepperoni	Pepperoni	Pepperoni

Now pepperoni pizza has 8 first-place votes, veggie pizza has 11, and sausage pizza has 7, so sausage pizza is eliminated to give a new preference schedule.

Number of students with this preference schedule	8	5	6	7
	Pepperoni	Veggie	Veggie	Veggie
	Veggie	Pepperoni	Pepperoni	Pepperoni

Now there is a run-off between pepperoni pizza and veggie pizza, with veggie pizza winning with 18 first-place votes against the 8 first-place votes for pepperoni pizza.

Consider This . . .

3. Use the Hare elimination procedure to determine a winning pizza from the vote your class held in Activity 2. Did you get the same result as with the first run-off procedure?

4. In your group, compare the plurality method, the standard run-off procedure, and the Hare elimination procedure. Decide which procedure you would recommend for your class to use in its next election.

Sequential Pairwise Election

Another variation of the run-off procedure is the **sequential pairwise** procedure. This method is used in the U.S. House of Representatives to vote on different options for the same bill. In the House, the method is referred to as **parliamentary procedure**. First, one pair of decision options is considered and a vote is taken; then the winner is paired with another option, and another vote is taken. This procedure of pairing and voting continues until a final winner is selected.

In a sequential run-off, the voters' preference schedules are used to simulate elections between randomly chosen pairs of candidates. Two candidates are chosen at random, and the preference schedules are used to determine which is the preferred candidate. The winner is then paired off with another randomly chosen candidate. The procedure of pairing off two candidates and voting between them continues until a winner emerges.

To hold a sequential pairwise run-off, the physics class starts by drawing the names of two pizza types out of a hat. The first two drawn are veggie pizza and sausage pizza. The class takes the original preference schedule and considers only the battle between veggie pizza and sausage pizza. They see that 19 out of 26 students preferred veggie pizza to sausage pizza. Next the students draw pepperoni pizza out of the hat, so pepperoni pizza is paired with veggie pizza. From the preference schedule, the students see that 18 out of 26 students preferred veggie pizza to pepperoni pizza. Next the students pair ham pizza and veggie pizza. They see that 20 out of 26 students preferred ham pizza to veggie pizza, so in the sequential pairwise run-off, ham pizza is the winner. The diagram below shows the results of this procedure.

Consider This . . .

5. You have explored three different run-off election decision procedures for the same election, and the results have been different each time. Discuss the following questions with your group.

    •   Which of the three types of run-off elections do you prefer? Why?

    •   How do you decide whether one method is fairer than another?

    •   Which procedure would you prefer to use for the pizza vote in your class?

6. Write a short paragraph recommending the procedure you think your class should use for its pizza selection. Be sure to justify your recommendation.

Explore Further

7. If there are *n* candidates in a sequential pairwise run-off, how many times would they have to be paired off to arrive at a winner?

8. Jacob is so enthusiastic about the run-off election procedures that he suggests that his family take a vote to decide which movie they will watch from Four Star Video's Classics of the Week list. Jacob's parents agree, and they vote between four movies: *Star Wars,*

Dances with Wolves, Sound of Music, and *Beauty and the Beast.* Their preference schedules are shown below.

Jacob	Mother	Father
Star Wars	Sound of Music	Dances with Wolves
Dances with Wolves	Star Wars	Beauty and the Beast
Beauty and the Beast	Dances with Wolves	Sound of Music
Sound of Music	Beauty and the Beast	Star Wars

- Is there a winner using the plurality method?

- Is there a winner using the standard run-off procedure? If so, what is it? If not, why not?

- Is there a winner using the Hare elimination procedure? If so, what is it? If not, why not?

9. Jacob and his parents decide to try using a sequential pairwise run-off procedure. First they draw *Star Wars* out of the hat, then *Dances with Wolves,* then *Sound of Music,* and finally *Beauty and the Beast.* Which movie wins?

10. Jacob's mother wonders if the order in which the movies were chosen matters, so they try it again. This time, they first pull *Beauty and the Beast* out of the hat, then *Sound of Music,* then *Dances with Wolves* and finally *Star Wars.* Which movie wins? Did the order matter?

11. The order of pairing off and voting between candidates is called an agenda.

- Can you find an agenda that results in *Sound of Music* winning?

- Can you find an agenda that leads to Dances with Wolves winning?

Research

12. Design an ordinal ballot for a survey on a topic of your choice. Collect responses from 20 or more people. Summarize the results of your survey using each run-off procedure. Be sure to save the ballots you collect, because you may want to use them in a later activity. (If you collected survey results in an earlier activity, you can use those ballots for this research question.)

TEACHER'S NOTES

Students will probably need more than one class period to complete this activity, and they will need the voting results from Activity 2.

This activity describes three run-off election procedures. To learn how each procedure works, students analyze the same results of a vote taken with ordinal ballots. For the election described in the activity, each procedure gives a different result. As students work through the activity, they work in their groups to apply the election procedures to the data from their own pizza election.

At the conclusion of the activity, have the groups present their recommendations of which procedure to use. Ask students to describe what they think are the strengths and drawbacks of the various methods and which method they think is fairest.

Answers

Consider This . . .

1–6. Answers will vary.

Explore Further

7. $n - 1$

8. • No. There is a three-way tie using the plurality method.

   • No. Using the standard run-off procedure, there are no two unique highest first-place vote-getters.

   • No. After you eliminate *Beauty and the Beast*, there is no unique lowest vote-getter.

9. *Beauty and the Beast* wins.

10. *Star Wars* wins. Yes, the order does matter in a sequential pairwise run-off.

11. There are several possible agendas. One agenda is given for each case.

   For *Sound of Music* to win, first choose *Dances with Wolves*, then *Star Wars*, then *Beauty and the Beast*, and then *Sound of Music*.

   For *Dances with Wolves* to win, first choose *Sound of Music*, then *Star Wars*, then *Dances with Wolves*, then *Beauty and the Beast*.

Research

12. Answers will vary.

CONDORCET'S ELECTION DECISION PROCEDURE

In Activity 3, you discovered a problem with some voting procedures. When Jacob and his family used the sequential pairwise run-off procedure, they found that the agenda, not the voters, determined the final decision! This is called the **agenda effect**. Mathematicians, political scientists, and politicians have all been interested in finding voting procedures that do not run the risk of the agenda effect.

The Marquis de Condorcet, an eighteenth-century mathematician, philosopher, and political analyst, proposed the following election decision procedure:

> Each pair of candidates should be considered in its own separate election and the winner determined. If one candidate emerges as the winner over all the others in these separate two-way contests, then that candidate is the voters' preferred choice.

"Can you believe it? Charlie the Chimp has won the election."

The physics class decided to re-examine their pizza vote using Condorcet's procedure. The results of their original vote are displayed below.

Number of students with this preference schedule	8	5	6	7
	Pepperoni	Ham	Veggie	Sausage
	Ham	Veggie	Ham	Ham
	Veggie	Sausage	Sausage	Veggie
	Sausage	Pepperoni	Pepperoni	Pepperoni

In order to use Condorcet's procedure, the students have to consider six two-way contests—pepperoni versus ham, pepperoni versus veggie, pepperoni versus sausage, ham versus veggie, ham versus sausage, and veggie versus sausage. For each of these contests, the students examine the preference schedules to see which pizza is the winner. Their results are summarized in the table below.

Pepperoni versus ham	Pepperoni Ham	8 votes 5 + 6 + 7 = **18 votes**
Pepperoni versus veggie	Pepperoni Veggie	8 votes 5 + 6 + 7 = **18 votes**
Pepperoni versus sausage	Pepperoni Sausage	8 votes 5 + 6 + 7 = **18 votes**
Ham versus veggie	Ham Veggie	8 + 5 + 7 = **20 votes** 6 votes
Ham versus sausage	Ham Sausage	8 + 5 + 6 = **19 votes** 7 votes
Veggie versus sausage	Veggie Sausage	8 + 5 + 6 = **19 votes** 7 votes

Because ham pizza beat each of the other three pizzas in a two-way race, the class declares it the winner.

You can use a **tournament graph** to illustrate the six two-way contests in this pizza election.

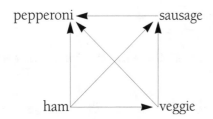

This type of diagram is also called a **digraph**, short for "directed graph." In the diagram, the line between two types of pizza indicates that there was a contest between them. The arrow points from the winner to the loser. You can use this diagram to rank the four candidates by counting the number of wins each type of pizza has.

From the digraph, you can see that ham pizza has three wins, veggie pizza has two wins, sausage pizza has one win, and pepperoni pizza has none. This information is summarized in the table below.

Pizza type	Number of wins
Ham	3
Veggie	2
Sausage	1
Pepperoni	0

Consider This . . .

1. Do you think Condorcet's procedure is fair? Discuss this in your group, using the following questions as guidelines.

   - How would you explain to pepperoni lovers that their pizza, which came in first using the plurality method, lost using this method?

   - Describe some of the positive aspects of Condorcet's procedure.

   - Describe any drawbacks there might be to Condorcet's procedure.

2. With your class, choose an issue with four choices to vote on. You might choose a political election, a field trip choice, or a school mascot choice, or you might vote to choose what topic you will vote on next time! Hold an election using ordinal ballots.

   - Analyze the results using Condorcet's election procedure. Which choice won?

   - Use a digraph to display the results of the election.

   - What percent of your classmates do you think are satisfied with the results of the election? What percent are dissatisfied?

   - Which choice would have won if you had used the plurality method?

   - Which of the election decision procedures you have learned about so far seems fairest?

Explore Further

3. The geology class has decided to use Condorcet's election procedure to determine the results of their field trip vote. Their vote is shown in the table below.

Number of students with this preference schedule	7	4	8	6	5
	Grand Canyon	Bryce Canyon	Death Valley	Death Valley	Grand Canyon
	Bryce Canyon	Grand Canyon	Bryce Canyon	Grand Canyon	Death Valley
	Death Valley	Death Valley	Grand Canyon	Bryce Canyon	Bryce Canyon

- Using Condorcet's procedure, which option will be the winner?

- Use a digraph to display the results of the vote. Make a table to show how many wins each choice has.

- Some of the students want to try the Hare elimination procedure. Which choice would be the winner using this procedure?

- Which procedure would you recommend the geology class use for their election? Why?

4. In a physical education class, the badminton group decided to hold a round robin tournament. In this kind of tournament, each player plays against every other player once.

   - If there are 18 students in the class, how many games would they have to play?

   - How many rounds would they have to play if there were 100 students? n students?

5. Jacob tried to use a run-off procedure in Activity 3 to choose a movie from Four Star Video's Classics of the Week list with his family. Since the run-off procedures ended in ties and the sequential pairwise election gave different results depending on the agenda, he now suggests that his family use their preference schedules to decide which movie they will watch, but this time they will use Condorcet's election decision procedure to determine the result. Jacob's parents agree. Their preference schedules are shown below. What is the result of their vote using Condorcet's procedure?

Jacob	Mother	Father
Star Wars	Sound of Music	Dances with Wolves
Dances with Wolves	Star Wars	Beauty and the Beast
Beauty and the Beast	Dances with Wolves	Sound of Music
Sound of Music	Beauty and the Beast	Star Wars

6. Explain why Condorcet's method does not cure the agenda effect.

7. In Question 3, you found that the preference schedules for the geology class field trip provide a Condorcet winner. Explain why any order chosen for the sequential pairwise method will always result in the same winner when there is a Condorcet winner.

8. The Social Science Department at Central City High is holding a "Your Vote Counts" contest. Classes in all departments have been asked to submit an entry related to the theme. Ms. Pat Riot's mathematics class submitted the following poster containing problems related to voting. See how many of the problems you can solve.

---

m & *n* Pizza Puzzlers

A. Condorcet's procedure requires that there be two-way contests between each pair of candidates. How many two-way contests are there in an election between five pizzas? Six pizzas? *n* pizzas?

B. What is the maximum number of wins a pizza can have in a two-way contest election with *n* pizzas? Investigate.

C. What is the minimum number of wins a pizza can have in a two-way contest election with *n* pizzas? Investigate.

D. What is the minimum number of wins that a pizza can have in order to win (have the highest number of wins in) a two-way contest election using Condorcet's election decision procedure with *n* candidates? Investigate.

E. What is the maximum number of winners in a two-way contest election with *n* pizzas? Investigate.

Research

9. Write a short biography of the Marquis de Condorcet.

10. Design an ordinal ballot for a survey on a topic of your choice. Collect responses from 20 or more people. Summarize the results of your survey using Condorcet's election decision procedure. Be sure to save the ballots you collected, because you may want to use them in a later activity. (If you collected survey results in an earlier activity, you can use those ballots for this research question.)

TEACHER'S NOTES

Students may be eager to explore an alternative election procedure, since each run-off procedure in Activity 3 yielded a different result.

This activity includes a brief exposure to **digraphs**. A digraph is a finite, nonempty set of points, called vertices, together with some directed edges joining pairs of these points. These directed edges are subject to one restriction: The initial and terminal vertices of a directed edge may not be the same. Digraphs are used in discrete mathematics. They can be used to represent networks of one-way streets, hierarchies of relationships, friendship relationships, and logical relationships.

Condorcet's method leads to some interesting problems, as does Borda's procedure, which is presented in Activity 5. These problems are presented in Question 8. Proofs for the puzzlers are included in the answers. Some of your students may be able to provide proofs, although the activity doesn't ask them to do so. You might want to ask students to come up with other puzzlers on their own.

Question 4 in Explore Further involves generating a formula for the sum of numbers from 1 to n. If your students haven't been exposed to this before, it can be a fun topic. The story, which is only a myth, is that Gauss as a young boy did not behave well in his math class. As punishment, his teacher told him to find the sum of the numbers from 1 to 100. Gauss quickly replied that the sum was 5050. The teacher then asked for the sum from 1 to 1000, and Gauss responded that the sum was 500,500. Supposedly, the teacher was not pleased with Gauss's precociousness! Gauss used a "trick" to see that the sum of the numbers from 1 to n is $\frac{n(n+1)}{2}$. You can find examples of Gauss's method in many standard algebra textbooks.

Answers

Consider This . . .

1. Answers will vary.

2. Answers will vary.

Explore Further

3. • The Grand Canyon will be the winner if Condorcet's method is used.

- The digraph should look like the one at right. The table below represents the information in the digraph.

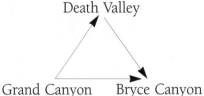

Death Valley

Grand Canyon   Bryce Canyon

Grand Canyon	2
Death Valley	0
Bryce Canyon	1

- Grand Canyon would be the winner using the sequential run-off procedure.

- Answers will vary.

4. With 18 students, there will be 153 matches. With 100 students, there will be 4950 matches. With n students, there will be $\frac{n(n-1)}{2}$ matches.

5. There is no winner. None of the movies beats all the others in the six two-way contests.

6. Whenever the agenda effect is present, Condorcet's method will not select a winner.

7. If a candidate is a Condorcet winner, it can beat every other candidate in a separate two-way contest. To hold a sequential pairwise run-off, regardless of the agenda chosen, the Condorcet winner at some point will be paired against another candidate in a two-way contest. Each time this happens, the Condorcet winner will win the two-way contest, thereby winning the sequential pairwise run-off.

8. A. With five pizzas there are $4 + 3 + 2 + 1 = 10$ winners; with six pizzas there are 15 winners; with n pizzas there are $\frac{n(n-1)}{2}$ winners.

   Proof: Each candidate participates in $n - 1$ two-way contests. The product $n(n - 1)$ counts each contest twice, so the total of two-way contests is given by $\frac{n(n-1)}{2}$.

   B. The maximum number of wins is $n - 1$.

   Proof: A candidate will receive the maximum number of wins when it wins each two-way contest in which it participates. Since each candidate is in $n - 1$ contests, $n - 1$ is the maximum number of wins. Note that only one candidate can have this maximum number of wins, since the other candidates must have lost to it, and their number of wins therefore cannot be $n - 1$.

   C. The minimum number of wins in a two-way contest election is 0.

   Proof: A candidate will have a minimum score if it loses all its two-way contests. Note that only one candidate can have this minimum, since all the other candidates must have won against it, and their scores therefore cannot also be zero.

   D. The minimum number of wins using Condorcet's election decision procedure is $\frac{(n-1)}{2}$.

Proof: Assume that the winner wins w of the two-way contests. Since there are $\frac{n(n-1)}{2}$ contests in all, the other candidates can win a combined total of $\frac{n(n-1)}{2} - w$ contests. Each of the other candidates can win no more than w contests, so their combined total must be less than $(n-1)w$. This leads to the inequality $(n-1)w \geq \frac{n(n-1)}{2} - w$, which can be simplified to $w \geq \frac{(n-1)}{2}$.

E. If n is odd, there can be n winners. If n is even, there can be at most $n-1$ winners.

    Proof: In puzzler A, you found that there are $\frac{n(n-1)}{2}$ contests that can be won. The average score per candidate can be found by dividing the total number of possible wins by the number of candidates to get $A = \frac{(n-1)}{2}$.

    If n is odd, A is an integer, and it is therefore possible that all n candidates have the same score. If n is odd, then A cannot be an integer, and all n candidates cannot have the same score. If one candidate's score is zero, though, it is possible that the other $(n-1)$ candidates are tied with the same score of $\frac{n}{2}$. Note that $\frac{n}{2}$ is an integer in this case, since n is even.

Research

9. Condorcet's (1743–1794) full name was Marie-Jean-Antoine-Nicolas Caritat de Condorcet. In the late eighteenth century, several new branches of mathematics had been created. These branches led to complicated problems for which no general solutions could be found, and prominent mathematicians such as Euler, d'Aemgert, and Lagrange believed that mathematics had almost exhausted its ideas; they saw no new great minds on the horizon. Condorcet was more optimistic. He believed that application and theory worked together, one inspiring the other, and he predicted that mathematics was only beginning to achieve its promise.

   In 1765, Condorcet wrote *Du calcul integral*, in which he tried unsuccessfully to create order out of all the various tricks and methods used to solve differential equations. Condorcet was also on the committee of the French Academy of Sciences, which set up the metric system.

10. Answers will vary.

BORDA'S ELECTION DECISION PROCEDURE

Jean-Charles Borda was born in Dax, France, on May 4, 1733. He was the tenth of 16 children. His parents were both members of the nobility, and his family had a history of serving in the military going back to the early seventeenth century. Borda became a major figure in the French navy and participated in the American Revolution as well as in many scientific voyages. In addition to his work in fluid mechanics and the development of instruments, he was one of the first to develop a mathematical theory of elections.

Being the tenth of sixteen children, Borda had lots of practice in perfecting his voting procedure.

Borda was concerned that the plurality method of election might select the wrong candidate. He suggested an alternative to Condorcet's election decision procedure, that he called "the method of marks." Borda suggested giving each candidate "marks" or "points" based on how well he or she did in each of the preference schedules. In an election between n candidates, the winner of each contest gets $n - 1$ points for being in first place. The second-place candidate gets $n - 2$ points, the third-place candidate gets $n - 3$ points, and so on down to the last-place candidate, who gets 0 points.

The physics class decided to try Borda's procedure in their pizza election. Their election was between four candidates, so for each preference schedule the first-place pizza gets 3 points, the second-place pizza 2 points, the third-place pizza 1 point, and the last-place pizza 0 points.

Number of students with this preference schedule	8	5	6	7
3	Pepperoni	Ham	Veggie	Sausage
2	Ham	Veggie	Ham	Ham
1	Veggie	Sausage	Sausage	Veggie
0	Sausage	Pepperoni	Pepperoni	Pepperoni

To assign the points, the physics class looked at the preference schedules. Pepperoni was the first choice of eight students and got 3 points from each of them. It was the fourth choice of five students with one preference schedule, the fourth choice of six students with a different preference schedule, and the fourth choice of seven more students with yet another preference schedule. Therefore, pepperoni pizza has a total of 24 points.

Vote count for pepperoni pizza: $8(3) + 5(0) + 6(0) + 7(0) = 24$

The other three pizzas receive points using the same process:

Vote count for ham pizza: $8(2) + 5(3) + 6(2) + 7(2) = 57$

Vote count for veggie pizza: $8(1) + 5(2) + 6(3) + 7(1) = 43$

Vote count for sausage pizza: $8(0) + 5(1) + 6(1) + 7(3) = 32$

Because ham pizza has the most points, the physics class once again declared it the winner. The choices can be ranked from high to low, using each candidate's "Borda count:" ham, veggie, sausage, and pepperoni. In this case, the ranking is the same as the ranking achieved using Condorcet's procedure.

Consider This . . .

Your mathematics teacher has offered your class the opportunity to choose one night a week on which she won't assign homework, if everyone can agree on the night. The choices are Monday, Tuesday, Wednesday, or Thursday. Take a class vote using ordinal ballots, and use Borda's election decision procedure to determine the result.

1. In your groups, discuss the results of the vote. Use the following questions as guidelines.

   • Were you satisfied with the results of the vote? Why or why not?

   • Explain why you think Borda's procedure is fair or not fair.

   • In what ways does Borda's procedure seem better or worse than Condorcet's procedure?

- How do the results using Condorcet's method compare to the results using plurality?

- Which procedure would you recommend using the next time your class takes a vote? Why?

Explore Further

2. In Activities 3 and 4, Jacob and his family tried to use run-off procedures and Condorcet's election decision procedure to determine which movie to watch. What is the result of the family vote using Borda's procedure? Does the procedure give a ranking and a winner?

Jacob	Mother	Father
Star Wars	Sound of Music	Dances with Wolves
Dances with Wolves	Star Wars	Beauty and the Beast
Beauty and the Beast	Dances with Wolves	Sound of Music
Sound of Music	Beauty and the Beast	Star Wars

3. Ms. Pat Riot's mathematics class decided that m and n pizza puzzlers were such fun that they came up with a few more!

More m & n Pizza Puzzlers

A. What is the maximum number of points a Borda winner can have in an election with n pizzas and m voters? Investigate.

B. What is the sum of all the Borda points for n pizzas and m voters? Investigate.

C. What is the minimum number of points a Borda winner can have with n pizzas and m voters? Investigate.

D. What is the minimum number of points a Borda candidate pizza can have with n pizzas and m voters? Can more than one candidate have this minimum score? Investigate.

E. What is the maximum number of Borda winners in an election with n candidates and m voters? Investigate.

---

4. Suppose that instead of using $n - 1$ points for first place in an n-candidate election, $n - 2$ for second place, and so on, you used p points for first place, q points for second place, r for third place, and so on, where $p > q > r > \ldots$. Will the relative rankings of the candidates change, or will they always remain the same? Investigate.

Calculator Exploration

5. If your calculator can do matrix operations, then you can easily compute the vote totals for the Borda's election decision procedure. Store the Borda points for the preference schedules in matrix A and the frequency of each schedule in matrix B. You would enter the pizza preference schedule and frequencies in matrices like those shown below. Each horizontal row in matrix A represents the point value for one type of pizza.

$$\begin{array}{c} P \\ H \\ V \\ S \end{array} \begin{bmatrix} 3 & 0 & 0 & 0 \\ 2 & 3 & 2 & 2 \\ 1 & 2 & 3 & 1 \\ 0 & 1 & 1 & 3 \end{bmatrix} \begin{bmatrix} 8 \\ 5 \\ 6 \\ 7 \end{bmatrix}$$

Be sure you understand why the numbers are arranged the way they are in the matrices, and then check that the product of these matrices provides the correct results. Use this method to explore possible results for Question 4.

Research

6. Design an ordinal ballot for a survey on a topic of your choice. Collect responses from 20 or more people. Summarize the results of your survey using Borda's election decision procedure. Be sure to save the ballots you collected, because you may want to use them in a later activity. (If you collected survey results in an earlier activity, you can use those ballots for this research question.)

TEACHER'S NOTES

In France during the late eighteenth century, there was a drive to apply the methods of rigorous and mathematical thought to the human sciences. Some of the more successful attempts were made in the field of political science by three French academicians: Borda, Condorcet, and Laplace. Their contributions were promptly lost for two centuries, but after being rediscovered in the 1950s, they now play a central role in the literature of public choice.

Jean-Charles Borda, in addition to his contributions to the mathematics of voting, was a brilliant physicist. His most important contributions were his work in fluid mechanics and his development and use of instruments for navigation, geodesy, and the determination of weights and measures.

Borda's election decision procedure is a variation of Condorcet's that involves assigning points to each candidate based on how well he or she does in each two-way contest. Borda's procedure leads to some interesting problems, which are presented in Question 3. Proofs for the puzzlers are included in the answers. Some of your students may be able to provide proofs, although the activity doesn't ask them to do so. You might want to ask students to come up with other puzzlers on their own.

Answers

Consider This . . .

1. Answers may vary. The results using Condorcet's method are the reverse of the results using plurality.

Explore Further

2. Using Borda's procedure, *Dances with Wolves* wins with 6 points. *Star Wars* gets 5 points, *Sound of Music* gets 4 points, and *Beauty and the Beast* gets 3 points.

3. A. The maximum number of points is $(n - 1)m$.

> **Proof:** A candidate would have the maximum Borda score if it is ranked highest in each of the preference schedules. In this case, there are m voters, each of whom gives the candidate $n - 1$ points.
> Note that only one candidate can have this score, because the other candidates must have been ranked lower and their score therefore cannot also be $(n - 1)m$.

B. The sum is $\frac{mn(n-1)}{2}$.

> **Proof**: The sum of all the Borda scores is given by
> $m(n-1) + m(n-2). \ldots + m(2) + m(1) + m(0)$, which simplifies to
> $m[(n-1) + (n-2) + \ldots + 2 + 1 + 0] = \frac{mn(n-1)}{2}$.

C. The minimum number of points is greater than $\frac{m(n-1)}{2}$.

> **Proof:** Assume that there is one winner whose score is w. In puzzler B, you found that the sum of
> all the scores of all the candidates is $\frac{mn(n-1)}{2}$, so the sum of the scores of the nonwinning
> candidates is $\frac{mn(n-1)}{2} - w$. Since the winner has w points, the score of each of the other
> $(n-1)$ candidates is less than w. Therefore, $(n-1)w > \frac{mn(n-1)}{2} - w$, which reduces to
> $w > \frac{m(n-1)}{2}$.

D. The minimum score is 0.

> **Proof:** A candidate would have the minimum score if it is ranked lowest by all m voters. Since the
> lowest ranking is worth zero Borda points, the minimum score is given by $0 \bullet m = m$. Note that
> only one person can have this score, because the other candidates must have been ranked higher
> and therefore their score cannot also be zero.

E. If either m is even or n is odd, there can be n winners. If m is odd and n is even,
there can be at most $n-1$ winners.

> **Proof:** In puzzler B above, you found that the sum of all the Borda scores is $\frac{mn(n-1)}{2}$. The
> average score per candidate is therefore $A = \frac{m(n-1)}{2}$. If either m is even or n is odd, A is
> an integer and it is therefore possible that all n candidates have the same score of A.

4. It turns out that the rankings will not necessarily always stay the same. Consider the
preference schedules from the physics class's pizza vote above. If a first-place position is
given 100 points, second place 3 points, third place 2 points, and fourth place 1 point,
then the resulting ranking is as follows:

Pepperoni: $8(100) + 5(1) + 6(1) + 7(1) = 818$

Ham: $8(3) + 5(100) + 6(3) + 7(3) = 563$

Veggie: $8(2) + 5(3) + 6(100) + 7(2) = 645$

Sausage: $8(1) + 5(2) + 6(2) + 7(100) = 730$

There is a completely different winner using this point system, and the ranking is in
reverse order of that of the original Borda ranking. This is actually the plurality ranking,
which can always be achieved by awarding the first-place position enough points.

Calculator Exploration

5. The resulting matrix should be $\begin{bmatrix} 24 \\ 57 \\ 43 \\ 32 \end{bmatrix}$. Other answers will vary.

Research

6. Answers will vary.

BLACK'S ELECTION DECISION PROCEDURE

Activities 4 and 5 introduced election decision procedures proposed by the Marquis de Condorcet and Jean Borda to determine the winner of an election. These two methods often produce similar results. But how can you determine a winner if the results are different? Condorcet and Borda had many discussions and often heated debates about which one of their methods produced the best results. The mathematician C. L. Dodgson, who was the author of *Alice in Wonderland* under the pseudonym Lewis Carroll, was also interested in election theory, in particular the paradoxes. He studied and wrote about the methods of Condorcet and Borda. Duncan Black, a twentieth-century English political scientist who was born in 1908 in Motherwell,

Little Duncan Black's favorite bedtime stories.

Scotland, rediscovered the works of Condorcet, Borda, and Dodgson. Black's work is the foundation of much of the subsequent research on election decision procedures. In 1958, Black wrote "The Theory of Committees and Elections." He also wrote a biography of Dodgson.

Consider This . . .

1. The board of a cooperative grocery store is attempting to decide between three different suppliers of organic produce. The suppliers differ in their price and also in the quality of their produce and the extent to which their products are organic. The board has decided that for financial reasons it is important to stick with one supplier.

   The three suppliers are Alpha Organics, Best Veggies, and Fine Fodder. The five board members decided to take a secret ballot using ordinal ballots. The results of their vote are shown below.

3	2
Alpha Organics	Best Veggies
Best Veggies	Fine Fodder
Fine Fodder	Alpha Organics

• Use the preference schedules to find the winner using Condorcet's procedure.

• Use the preference schedules to determine the winner using Borda's procedure.

• Compare the results of Condorcet's and Borda's procedures. Discuss with your group how you would advise the board to resolve the conflict.

Black suggested reconciling the methods of Condorcet and Borda by following this procedure: If there is a Condorcet winner, choose him or her. If there is no Condorcet winner, choose the Borda winner. In the case of the cooperative grocery store, Alpha Organics would be chosen as the supplier.

Another solution, proposed in 1907 by Australian E. J. Nanson, is to use a method called "Borda elimination." First, compute the Borda points. Then remove the candidate with the lowest Borda count and recompute the Borda points. Continue this process until a winner is determined. In the example above, after the first round Alpha Organics has 6 points, Best Veggies has 7 points, and Fine Fodder has 2 points. Eliminate Fine Fodder, since it received the fewest Borda points. The preference schedules now look like this:

3	2
Alpha Organics	Best Veggies
Best Veggies	Alpha Organics

Recompute the Borda points. Alpha Organics now has 3 points, and Best Veggies has 2 points, so Alpha Organics wins. In this example, Borda elimination produces the same results as the Condorcet method.

2. The senior orchestra at Central City High is planning an event to celebrate winning the All State Competition. Three possibilities have been proposed: a trip to the local amusement park, an all-night dance, and a trip to the city to hear a concert. The orchestra determined that each of the three choices would cost about the same, so they decided to take a vote. Their votes are shown in the preference schedules below.

8	11	12	20	16
Amusement park	Concert	Concert	Amusement park	Dance
Dance	Amusement park	Dance	Concert	Amusement park
Concert	Dance	Amusement park	Dance	Concert

- Use Borda elimination to determine the winning choice.

- Use Black's proposal to determine the winner.

3. Compare the results obtained using each of the four methods (Condorcet's, Borda's, Black's, and Borda elimination) with the preference schedules in the example and those in Question 1. Try to generalize about when these methods will give the same result. When they don't give the same result, which method seems fairest?

Explore Further

4. Ultimate Frisbee is a growing sport at Central City High. The Ultimate Club is sponsoring a weekend event, and each participant will receive a tee-shirt. The team decided to have the participants vote on the color of the tee-shirt. Team members collected the ballots and tabulated them. The results are shown in the preference schedules below.

12	7	20	18	23	25
Fuchsia	Fuchsia	Eggshell	Purple	Teal	Watermelon
Purple	Teal	Purple	Eggshell	Purple	Teal
Eggshell	Purple	Watermelon	Teal	Eggshell	Fuchsia
Watermelon	Eggshell	Fuchsia	Fuchsia	Watermelon	Purple
Teal	Watermelon	Teal	Watermelon	Fuchsia	Eggshell

- Determine the winner of the election by the plurality method. To do this, consider only the first-place votes.

- What percentage of the first-place votes did the winner receive?

- Use Black's method to determine the winning tee-shirt color. Is there a Condorcet winner?

- Use Borda elimination to determine the winning tee-shirt color.

5. The Ultimate Club has decided to provide a few hours of entertainment during their weekend event. The club has narrowed down the options to four possibilities: frisbee dog tricks, film clips of great ultimate games, an outdoor concert, and a demonstration of special frisbee techniques. The members of the club voted using ordinal ballots. The preference schedules below show the results of their vote.

8	3	14	13	6
Dog tricks	Dog tricks	Film clips	Outdoor concert	Technique demo
Film clips	Technique demo	Outdoor concert	Dog tricks	Film clips
Outdoor concert	Outdoor concert	Dog tricks	Techn ique demo	Dog tricks
Technique demo	Film clips	Technique demo	Film clips	Outdoor concert

- Use Black's method to determine the winner. Is there a Condorcet winner?

- Use Borda elimination to determine the winner. If you have a programmable calculator, you can use matrices to do the computations at each stage.

- Compare the results using Black's method and Borda elimination. What choice would you recommend the Ultimate Club make?

6. There is a theorem that states that if there is a Condorcet winner, Borda elimination will always choose it. Give an explanation of why this is the case.

Research

7. Design an ordinal ballot for a survey on a topic of your choice. Collect responses from 20 or more people. (If you did a survey in a previous activity, you can use those results for this activity.) Analyze the results of your survey using Black's and Nanson's proposals. Did both procedures produce the same results? If not, which result more accurately reflects the results of your survey?

● TEACHER'S NOTES

Duncan Black studied at the University of Glasgow and spent most of his teaching career at the University College of North Wales, Bangor. He worked in the 1940s to develop a pure science of politics as a ramified theory of committees so that political science would be on the same kind of theoretical footing as economics.

Encourage your students to use matrices to compute the Borda scores for Borda's method and Borda elimination. It might be helpful for students to first write up the matrices and then enter them into their calculators.

Answers

Consider This . . .

1. • Using Condorcet's procedure, Alpha Organics wins each two-way contest and is therefore the winner.

   • Using Borda's method, each supplier receives the following Borda score:

Alpha Organics:	$3(2) + 2(0) = 6$
Best Veggies:	$3(1) + 2(2) = 7$
Fine Fodder:	$3(0) + 2(1) = 2$

   Using Borda's method, Best Veggies is the winner.

   • Answers will vary.

2. • Using Borda elimination, the amusement park wins.

   • Using Black's method, the amusement park is the Condorcet winner.

3. For Question 1, the winners are:

   Alpha Organics (Condorcet)

   Best Veggies (Borda)

   Alpha Organics (Black)

   Alpha Organics (Borda elimination)

   For Question 2, the amusement park wins using any method. Other answers will vary.

Explore Further

4. • Watermelon wins using the plurality method.

   • The winner received 23.8% of first-place votes.

   • Purple wins using Black's method. There is no Condorcet winner.

   • Purple wins using Borda elimination.

5. • Using Black's method, the dog tricks option will win. There is no Condorcet winner, and the dog tricks option wins using Borda's method.

   • Using Borda elimination, the film clips option wins. Using matrices, the process looks like this:

   First round:
   $$\begin{bmatrix} 3 & 3 & 1 & 2 & 1 \\ 2 & 0 & 3 & 0 & 2 \\ 1 & 1 & 2 & 3 & 0 \\ 0 & 2 & 0 & 1 & 3 \end{bmatrix} \begin{bmatrix} 8 \\ 3 \\ 14 \\ 13 \\ 6 \end{bmatrix} = \begin{bmatrix} 79 \\ 70 \\ 81 \\ 37 \end{bmatrix}$$

   In this round, the technique demo option has the fewest points and is eliminated.

   Second round:
   $$\begin{bmatrix} 2 & 2 & 0 & 1 & 1 \\ 1 & 0 & 2 & 0 & 2 \\ 0 & 1 & 1 & 2 & 0 \end{bmatrix} \begin{bmatrix} 8 \\ 3 \\ 14 \\ 13 \\ 6 \end{bmatrix} = \begin{bmatrix} 41 \\ 48 \\ 43 \end{bmatrix}$$

   In this round, the dog tricks option has the fewest points and is eliminated.

   Third round:
   $$\begin{bmatrix} 1 & 0 & 1 & 0 & 1 \\ 0 & 1 & 0 & 1 & 0 \end{bmatrix} \begin{bmatrix} 8 \\ 3 \\ 14 \\ 13 \\ 6 \end{bmatrix} = \begin{bmatrix} 28 \\ 16 \end{bmatrix}$$

   In this round, the outdoor concert option has the fewest points and is eliminated, leaving the film clips option as the winner.

   • Answers will vary.

6. Suppose candidate X is a Condorcet winner; then X beats every other candidate in a two-way contest. This means that for each candidate X is ranked above that candidate more than X is ranked below that candidate. This means that the X appears, on average, more than halfway up all the preference schedules, so X has a higher-than-average Borda count. This in turn means that X will never have the lowest Borda count and will therefore never be eliminated using Borda elimination.

Research

7. Answers will vary.

SINGLE TRANSFERABLE VOTE

An election decision procedure that is sometimes used when more than one candidate is to be elected is called the **single transferable vote** (STV). It is also called **preferential voting**. This method was first proposed in the 1850s by Thomas Hare, an English barrister, and Carl Andrae, a Danish mathematician. When you use this method to elect a single winner, the results are the same as those you get using the Hare elimination method in Activity 3. The single transferable vote method is used to elect public officials in Australia, Malta, and the Republic of Ireland; for local city council elections

All right, we eliminated George and Julie, we transferred votes to Linda and Susan, and we distributed all the surplus votes to the remaining candidates. Who do you show winning this time?

in Cambridge, Massachusetts; and for local school board elections in New York City. Preferential voting is often used in elections for school or university boards, city councils, and club committees, as well as for electing officials in professional and other organizations. It is the method used to select nominees for the movie industry's Academy Awards.

One reason for choosing a method such as the single transferable vote is to assure proportional representation of the voting constituency. For example, a school board might need to be chosen to represent a diverse neighborhood consisting of a variety of ethnic and religious groups. If the plurality method is used, it's quite possible that the winning slate will represent only the group with the largest number of voters. An advantage of the single transferable vote method for the voter is that if your vote doesn't help elect your first-choice candidate, it will be counted toward one of your lower choices.

To use the single transferable vote method, each voter must complete an ordinal ballot, listing the candidates in order of preference. The first-choice votes are tabulated, and candidates who achieve a prescribed quota of votes are declared elected. If a candidate receives more first-choice votes than the quota, the surplus of votes is transferred proportionally to the other candidates. (The details of how votes are actually transferred differ from one system to another.) If no candidate at a given stage has a quota and there are more seats to be assigned, the lowest vote getter is eliminated, and the ballots for this candidate are transferred, as in the sequential run-off, to other candidates. The process continues until all the seats are filled. The diagram below will help you understand this process.

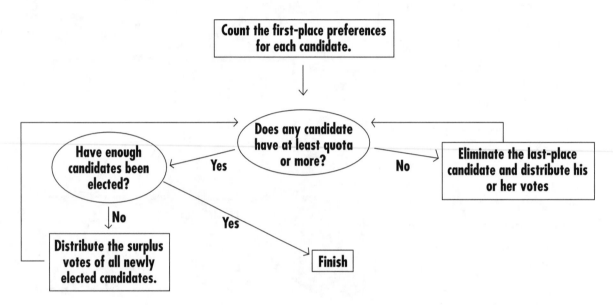

The quota is usually defined this way: If there are s seats to be filled by n available candidates, where $n > s$, and the number of voters is m, then the quota is given by $Q = \left[\dfrac{m}{s+1}\right] + 1$. (The brackets indicate the greatest integer.)

The single transferable vote method could be used to elect two representatives to a countywide residents' association. There are 23 voters in the Midlands residents' association, 13 Conservatives and 10 Liberals. The Conservative candidates are Winston and Nadia, with Winston the more conservative of the two. The Liberal candidates are Theo and Rudy, with Rudy the more radical of the two. In a vote for representatives to the countywide residents' association, using ordinal ballots, the following preference schedules emerged.

Conservative		Liberal	
7	**6**	**6**	**4**
Winston	Nadia	Theo	Rudy
Nadia	Winston	Rudy	Theo
Theo	Theo	Nadia	Nadia
Rudy	Rudy	Winston	Winston

To use the single transferable vote method, first compute the quota. In this case, $Q = \left\lceil \frac{23}{2+1} \right\rceil + 1 = 8$. None of the candidates received the quota of first-place votes, so the lowest vote-getter, Rudy, is eliminated. The votes of Rudy's four supporters are transferred to Theo, their second choice, giving these new preference schedules.

Conservative		Liberal
7	**6**	**10**
Winston	Nadia	Theo
Nadia	Winston	Nadia
Theo	Theo	Winston

Theo now has two votes more than the quota, and he is elected. Theo's two surplus votes are transferred to Nadia, resulting in these preference schedules.

Conservative	
7	**8**
Winston	Nadia
Nadia	Winston
Theo	Theo

Nadia has now reached the quota, and she is elected to the remaining seat.

Consider This . . .

1. Compare the result using the single transferable vote method to the result using Hare's sequential run-off method for the Midlands residents' association. Which result seems to best represent the wishes of the voters?

2. If the size of the residents' association were increased so that Midlands could elect three representatives, which candidates would be elected using the single transferable vote method?

3. If the size were decreased so that Midlands was allowed only one representative, who would be elected using the single transferable vote?

Explore Further

4. Just before the latest election was held in Midlands, three students turned 18 and became eligible to vote. An election was held, with the same candidates, resulting in the following preference schedules. Which two candidates would be elected using the single transferable vote method?

9	6	2	4	5
Winston	Theo	Rudy	Rudy	Nadia
Nadia	Rudy	Theo	Theo	Theo
Theo	Nadia	Nadia	Nadia	Rudy
Rudy	Winston	Winston	Winston	Winston

5. What would have been the results of the election if two voters who preferred Rudy to Theo changed their minds and preferred Theo to Rudy? Use the new preference schedules to determine the two winning candidates.

9	6	2	4	5
Winston	Theo	Theo	Rudy	Nadia
Nadia	Rudy	Rudy	Theo	Theo
Theo	Nadia	Nadia	Nadia	Rudy
Rudy	Winston	Winston	Winston	Winston

6. Compare the results of the elections in Questions 4 and 5. What do you notice? Do you think it is fair?

7. The town of Smytheville, with 1608 voters, held an election for two positions on the city council, that resulted in the preference schedules shown below. Which candidates would be elected using the single transferable vote method? (You will need to decide how to allot the extra votes after the first round.) Be sure to explain your method. Do you think the results are fair? Why or why not?

417	74	121	365	285	346
Anders	Anders	Kristina	Kristina	Marie	Marie
Kristina	Marie	Anders	Marie	Anders	Kristina
Marie	Kristina	Marie	Anders	Kristina	Anders

Research

8. Find out about some places or organizations where the single transferable vote method is used or has been used in the past. See if you can find out why this method was chosen or why it is no longer used. You may find it helpful to research the term "preferential voting."

9. Different methods are used to "transfer" votes in applying the single transferable vote method. Find out about at least one of these methods and provide an example to show how the method works.

TEACHER'S NOTES

The single transferable vote seems to provide voters with a way of fully expressing their preferences, ensuring maximum and equitable consideration of each voter's preferences. This method, however, is subject to four different paradoxes. In "Paradoxes of Preferential Voting," Peter Fishburn and Steven Brams summarize them:

- No-show paradox: The addition of identical ballots with candidate X ranked last may change the winner from another candidate to X.

- Thwarted-majorities paradox: A candidate who can defeat every other candidate in direct-comparison majority votes may lose the election.

- Multiple-districts paradox: A candidate can win in each district separately yet lose the general election in the combined districts.

- More-is-less paradox: If the winner was ranked higher by some voters, with all else unchanged, another candidate might have won.

One of these paradoxes is uncovered in Question 6. If you have students who are interested in further reading, they may enjoy Fishburn and Brams's article in *Mathematics Magazine*. It is presented in a way that makes it accessible to many high school students.

Answers

Consider This . . .

1. Using Hare's sequential run-off method, Winston and Theo win. Answers may vary as to which result better represents the wishes of the voters, but Nadia is rated above Winston on three of the four different preference schedules.

2. With three seats, the quota is $Q = \left[\frac{23}{3+1}\right] + 1 = 6$. So Winston, Nadia, and Theo all meet the quota and are elected.

3. With only one seat, the quota is 12. All four candidates fall short, so Rudy is eliminated, which gives the three-column preference schedule in the example. But all three remaining candidates still fall short of the quota, so Nadia is eliminated, and her 6 votes are transferred to Winston, who is then elected.

Explore Further

4. The quota with 26 voters will be $Q = \left[\frac{26}{2+1}\right] + 1 = 9$. Since Winston has reached the quota, he is elected. Winston has no surplus votes, so Nadia, who is the lowest first-place vote-getter, is eliminated, and her 5 votes are transferred to Theo, giving the following preference schedules.

11	2	4
Theo	Rudy	Rudy
Rudy	Theo	Theo

Theo is elected with 11 votes.

5. In this case, Winston is immediately elected again, with no surplus votes to transfer. This time Rudy is the lowest vote-getter. Rudy's four votes are transferred to Nadia, who now meets the quota with 9 votes.

6. The results of the elections in Questions 4 and 5 are paradoxical. The only difference in the preference schedules is that in the second election two voters changed Theo from their second to their first choice. This had the strange result of denying him the election! It doesn't seem fair that a candidate can lose an election because he or she received too many first-place votes and would in fact have won if some voters had voted for him as their second choice rather than their first. Fishburn and Brams (1983) call this the "more-is-less" paradox.

7. The quota is 537. In the first round, Marie is elected with 631 votes. She has a surplus of 94 votes, which are distributed in proportion to Anders and Kristina. One way to do this is to give Kristina $\frac{346}{631} \cdot 94 \approx 52$ more votes. Anders would receive $\frac{285}{631} \cdot 94 \approx 42$ votes. Kristina now has 486 + 52 = 538 votes, which is one more vote than the quota, so she is elected.

Research

8. Answers will vary.

9. Answers will vary. The differences are usually in the methods used to distribute the votes proportionally.

ARROW'S THEOREM AND APPROVAL VOTING

In the previous activities, you examined various election decision procedures. Each procedure is designed to choose one or more candidates from a slate of three or more. You found that each procedure has some democratic features but can give different results in considering the same voters with the same preference schedules.

Kenneth Arrow, an economist, tackled the problem of deciding the fairest election procedure for determining the winner of an election. He reached the conclusion that any democratic voting system that ranks all the candidates can give undemocratic results. This was regarded as a "devastating discovery,"[1] and it led to his winning the Nobel Prize in economics in 1972.

Arrow was interested in mathematically analyzing election procedures that rank the candidates. He made a list of important features that determine the fairness of an election procedure. Among the fairness criteria that Arrow defined were the following:

- There should be no dictator. A voter is an Arrow dictator when other people's preference rankings are irrelevant to the outcome. In other words, for any two candidates A and B, there is no individual voter such that whenever he or she prefers A to B, A is always preferred to B.

- If every voter prefers one candidate over another, then society should also prefer that candidate.

- The election decision procedure used should not encourage voters to lie about their true preferences.

The last Arrow criterion may seem surprising. It is the sort of unexpected result that shows up when mathematicians start to experiment with a problem.

The physical education class has decided to take a vote to decide which activity they will have for PE for the next quarter. Their choices are aerobics, badminton, football, or softball. They took a vote using ordinal ballots, and their preference schedules are shown below.

Number of students with this preference schedule	12	5	10	11
	Aerobics	Badminton	Football	Softball
	Badminton	Football	Badminton	Badminton
	Football	Softball	Softball	Football
	Softball	Aerobics	Aerobics	Aerobics

Consider This . . .

1. Use Borda's election decision procedure to determine which activity the PE class chose by ranking the activities based on the number of points they got.

2. The ten students who wanted football as their first choice decided to try a different voting strategy. Instead of voting their true preferences, they voted for the activities in this order: football, softball, aerobics, and badminton. How did this strategy affect the results?

3. In response to the observation that his method is not strategy-proof, Borda commented, "My scheme is only intended for honest men."[2] Describe in your own words the flaw that you have discovered in Borda's method.

> In all, Arrow listed five fairness criteria for an election method. Based on these criteria, Arrow formulated and proved the following theorem in his book *Social Values and Individual Choice*:
>
> > There does not exist an election procedure which ranks for society three or more candidates based on individual preferences, and which obeys the five fairness conditions.
>
> Despite the gloomy prediction of Arrow's theorem, social-choice theorists continue to try to invent better voting methods that will overcome or minimize the flaws of known voting methods. One such voting method is called **approval voting**. It is particularly well suited to elections with several candidates. When you vote using approval voting, you give any candidate you approve of a vote. There is no limit on how many candidates you can vote for. If you disapprove of a candidate, you don't vote for him or her. The winner is the candidate who receives the most approval votes. This system also

works well in elections in which more than one candidate can win, for example, in elections of new members to the Baseball Hall of Fame or committee members to the American Mathematical Society.

4. The physical education class decided to use approval voting to choose the PE activity for the next quarter. All of the students approve of their top two choices except the football players. They only approve of football. Add up the approval votes each activity received and record them in the table below. Which activity wins using approval voting?

Activity	Number of approval votes
Aerobics	
Badminton	
Football	
Softball	

5. Use approval voting to take a class vote on one of the issues you have voted on in the previous six activities (pizza choice, night off from homework, or some other issue) and analyze the results.

   • Are you satisfied with the result?

   • Does this method seem more or less fair than other methods you have explored so far?

   • Do you think approval voting is subject to the same problems that affect the results using Borda's method? Discuss any other problems that you think might affect the fairness of the results when using approval voting.

Explore Further

6. In Activity 6, Central City's Ultimate Club voted on tee-shirt colors, resulting in the following preference schedules. The club decided to have a revote using approval voting. When the ballots were returned, everyone approved of their first choice. In addition, the 7 participants who chose fuchsia as their first choice also approved of teal, and the 25 participants who chose watermelon approved of every color except eggshell. Which color will win using approval voting?

12	7	20	18	23	25
Fuchsia	Fuchsia	Eggshell	Purple	Teal	Watermelon
Purple	Teal	Purple	Eggshell	Purple	Teal
Eggshell	Purple	Watermelon	Teal	Eggshell	Fuchsia
Watermelon	Eggshell	Fuchsia	Fuchsia	Watermelon	Purple
Teal	Watermelon	Teal	Watermelon	Fuchsia	Eggshell

7. Make a chart summarizing the election decision procedures you have studied in the previous activities.

8. Create a scenario that involves using an election decision procedure. Which procedure would you recommend be used for your scenario? Why?

9. Trade scenarios with one of your classmates. Each of you should analyze the other's scenario and recommend an election decision procedure. Compare your results when you are done. Did you agree?

10. Based on what you have learned in these activities, what changes would you recommend in the voting methods used in primary and general elections in the United States?

Research

11. Do some research and find out more about approval voting. What are some of the advantages and criticisms of this method?

● TEACHER'S NOTES

This activity introduces students to Arrow's theorem, which states that any conceivable democratic voting system can yield undemocratic results. Paul Samuelson, who later won the Nobel Memorial Prize in economic sciences, described Arrow's theorem:

> The search of the great minds of recorded history for the perfect democracy, it turns out, is the search for a chimera, for a logical self-contradiction. Now scholars all over the world—in mathematics, politics, philosophy and economics—are trying to salvage what can be salvaged from Arrow's devastating discovery that is to mathematical politics what Kurt Gödel's 1931 impossibility-of-proving-consistency theorem is to mathematical logic.[3]

In the Consider This section, students explore the criterion that an election decision procedure should not encourage voters to lie about their true preferences.

In the second part of the activity, students are introduced to approval voting. Have your students take a vote using approval voting on one of the issues they have voted on in a previous activity.

Answers

● Consider This . . .

1. Badminton: 119

   Football: 101

   Softball: 86

   Aerobics: 74

2. Football: 101

   Softball: 96

   Baseball: 88

   Aerobics: 84

3. The students who prefer football can manipulate the vote by lying about their true preferences.

4. Badminton wins when approval voting is used. This is the same result as the first result using Borda's method.

5. Answers will vary. Approval voting suffers from the same flaw as Borda's method in that it is subject to strategic manipulation, but it is no more vulnerable to insincere voting than other known methods.

Explore Further

6. Teal wins.

7. Answers will vary.

8. Answers will vary.

9. Answers will vary.

10. Answers will vary.

Research

11. Answers will vary.

   According to Brams and Fishburn,[4] these are some of the advantages and criticisms of approval voting:

   ## Advantages

   - It gives voters more flexible options. They can vote for a single favorite, or they can vote for more than one choice.

   - It could increase voter turnout because voters would feel as if they were better able to express their preferences.

   - It would help elect the candidate with the strongest overall support.

   - It would support minority candidates. Voters often do not vote for their first choice because they don't think that candidate has a chance of winning.

   - It is relatively insensitive to the number of candidates running.

   ## Criticisms

   - It could encourage the proliferation of candidates.

   - It could undermine and possibly destroy the American two-party system.

Reference Notes

1. Hoffman, *Archimedes' Revenge* (1988).

2. *The New Palgrave: A Dictionary of Economics*, p. 263.

3. Hoffman, *op. cit.*

4. Brams and Fishburn, *Approval Voting* (1983).

APPORTIONMENT

Issues related to apportionment have been the subject of many political debates in the United States as well as in other countries. In the United States government, there are two representative bodies, the Senate and the House of Representatives. The Senate consists of two senators from each state, which means that each state is represented equally. The House of Representatives is designed to represent each state in proportion to its population. Since the ratification of the

This book will help you learn about apportioning the new all-county student council.

Constitution, politicians have struggled with the problem of determining a fair method for apportioning representatives from each state.

The students of Broad County faced the same problem when they were asked to help design a representative body consisting of students from each high school in the county. The students at Central City High School felt that this student council should represent the students by population so that each student in the county would be represented equally. The students at Outland High disagreed. They felt that there should be the same number of representatives from each school on the countywide student council so that the schools would be represented equally. The population of each school is given in the table below.

Activity	Student population
Central City High	4464
East High	3782
West High	3284
Hill High	1842
Outland High	1288
Sticks High	422

Consider This . . .

1. In which of the county schools do you think the students will prefer a system of representation based on a set number of representatives per school? In which schools will the students probably prefer a system of representation based on student populations?

2. What would you recommend as a system of representation for the Broad County student council? Is there a way to please everyone?

> The students finally decided that in their countywide student council the number of representatives from each school should be proportional to the number of students in the school. The next problem they have to solve is how to determine the number of representatives from each school that should be on the council.

> The administration of the school district has determined that there should be 30 or fewer students on the student council.

> Have each group in your class represent an apportionment committee for a different school in Broad County. As a member of the apportionment committee, your job is to decide how you would apportion the membership of the Broad County student council and prepare a report justifying your apportionment method.

3. Describe your method of apportionment for the Broad County student council.

4. Explain why you think your method of apportionment is fair. Will all schools be satisfied? Why or why not?

5. Present your results to the class and compare them with those of the other groups. Did all groups propose the same method of apportionment?

Explore Further

6. Wide County, which is adjacent to Broad County, has only one high school. Because many of the students at Wide High socialize with students from Broad County and are interested in the same issues that affect their friends, they want their school to be represented in the newly formed student council. There are 2478 students at Wide High. The administration is not prepared to add any representatives to the student council. However, they agree that Wide High should be allowed to join the Broad County student council. Calculate the student population percentages if Wide High is included and make recommendations for the number of representatives from each school. Describe the method you use for apportionment.

7. Which school's apportionment is most affected by the addition of Wide High?

8. Some of the students feel that the administration shouldn't limit the size of the student council. Experiment with different student council sizes to find a size that you would recommend. Make a proposal to the administration on how to create a student council on which membership is proportional to the population of the schools for the size of the council you recommend. Do you feel that this is a more reasonable way to approach the problem? Why or why not?

Calculator Exploration

9. If your calculator has a list function, you can enter the populations into a list and perform calculations on all entries in the list simultaneously. Try this, and explain how you could use this feature to help apportion the student council members.

Research

10. Read Article I, Section 2 of the U.S. Constitution. How did the framers of the Constitution say the population of the United States should be represented? How did representation relate to taxation? How do you think this affected debate about the fairness of apportionment?

11. When and how was it decided that we should have a Senate and a House of Representatives? What was the rationale behind the decision?

12. Find out what the electoral college is and how it works. Are all voters in the United States represented equally in the electoral college? Why was it created?

13. What are the sizes of the House of Representatives and the Senate? Are these sizes fixed, or are they allowed to grow in response to population changes?

TEACHER'S NOTES

This activity is the first one dealing with apportionment. Students are introduced to the basic principles of apportionment and are provided with some historical background. For the Consider This part of this activity, assign at least one group to represent each school so that all schools have a group watching out for their best interests. You may have an interesting debate over apportionment methods if the students take their parts to heart. If students use a percentage method, they will have to struggle with what to do with fractional representatives. They may also find that some schools are underrepresented. The framers of the U.S. Constitution realized that they had to require that each state be given at least one representative. Many students may devise a method very similar to Hamilton's method, which is presented in Activity 10.

Answers

Consider This . . .

1. The smaller schools would probably prefer a student government modeled after the Senate, and larger schools would probably prefer a model like the House of Representatives.

2. Answers will vary.

3–5. Answers will vary.

Explore Further

6. The apportionments students generate may vary. Ask them to describe their methods and verify that their results fit the method.

7. Answers may vary, based on the method of apportionment the students use. In general, the larger schools will experience larger percentage in apportionment changes by the addition of the new school.

8. Answers will vary.

Calculator Exploration

9. As the activities progress, students will be encouraged to use calculators to help with computation. One way to do this activity using the list function in some of the TI calculators follows.

    Students can enter the population of each school in L1 and then use the one-variable statistics function to find the sum of the populations.

    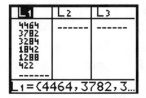

    Your students may be curious about the values the calculator displays. Encourage them to explore what the various values mean. They may even want to try to use some of these values in developing an apportionment method. Another way to find the sum of the populations is to use the sum command under the LIST MATH menu.

    Percentages can be calculated by entering L1/15082 into L2 (or L1/sum L1).

    To see the results, press ENTER.

    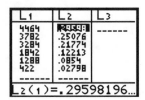

    Students can then compute the apportionment using strict percentages by entering L2 • 30 in L3. They will still have to determine how to allocate fractions of representatives.

    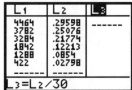

Research

10. Article I, Section 2 of the Constitution states:

Representatives and direct Taxes shall be apportioned among the several States which may be included within this Union, according to their respective Numbers, which shall be determined by adding to the whole Number of free Persons, including those bound to Service for a Term of Years, and excluding Indians not taxed, three fifths of all other Persons. The actual Enumeration shall be made within three years after the first meeting of the Congress of the United States, and within every subsequent Term of ten Years, in such manner as they shall by Law direct. The Number of Representatives shall not exceed one for every thirty thousand, but each State shall have at least one Representative.

11. The Constitutional Convention of 1787 formulated what is known as the "great compromise." This compromise established a representative branch of government composed of two houses.

12. The electoral college was born from a distrust of ordinary citizenry. The electoral college is a group of electors from each state. Electors were originally chosen by state legislatures, but soon this was changed so that they are now chosen by popular vote. The number of electors from each state is equal to the number of senators plus the number of representatives for that state.

13. The House is made up of 435 representatives, and the Senate has 100 members. The House size has varied in response to population growth. The Senate has also grown, but each state always has just two senators.

ALEXANDER HAMILTON'S METHOD OF APPORTIONMENT

Although the writers of the U.S. Constitution required that states be represented in proportion to their populations, they didn't prescribe a method for accomplishing this task. Because of this, there have often been long and heated debates over which method or rule should be used for apportioning members to the House of Representatives. Political concerns such as the conflicts between northern and southern states and between industrial and agricultural interests have influenced

During the founding of this nation there were many heated debates over which apportionment method should be used.

apportionment decisions. Overall population growth and shifts in population from one part of the country to another can also affect apportionment. Each state wants to protect its own interests and ensure that it is fairly represented, but it is difficult to find a method of apportionment that is fair to both large and small states. Many politicians have used creative mathematics in their struggle to ensure that their own states are fairly represented.

The first apportionment method to emerge from the struggle was Hamilton's method, sometimes referred to as the method of **greatest remainders**. Alexander Hamilton, first U.S. Secretary of the Treasury, first proposed this method in 1792. After a lengthy debate, President George Washington vetoed the bill that would have made this method law. Hamilton's method was reintroduced in 1850 as the Vinton method and was adopted. It was used to apportion the U.S. House of Representatives from 1850 until 1901, and today this method is used in Costa Rica, the Swiss National Council, and for the federal parts of Sweden's one house. It was also the method defined in the South African Interim Constitution for its general election of April 1994.

Hamilton's method works this way.

- First, choose a House size and a ratio of representation. (In the United States, these decisions are made by the existing House and Senate.) The ratio of representation determines how many people are to be represented by each member of the House. The U.S. Constitution specifies that 30,000 is the minimum ratio of people to representatives.

- The next step is to multiply the ratio of representation for each state by the population of the state to find the ideal quota for each state. Often these ideal quotas have fractional values, so they can't be used as they are because the number of representatives must be a whole number.

- Assign each state a number of seats equal to the integer part of its ideal quota. The Constitution guarantees that each state will have at least one representative, so if a state has an ideal quota less than one, assign it one representative.

- Find the sum of the number of seats assigned using the integer parts of the ideal quotas. If the total number of seats is not equal to the number of seats allowed, compare the fractional parts of each ideal quota. Assign the state with the largest fractional part one more seat. If a state was given a seat because its ideal quota was less than one, it doesn't qualify for an additional seat. Repeat this process until you have filled all the remaining seats. Thus, additional representatives are allotted to states with the "greatest remainders."

Hamilton and his followers decided that the House of Representatives should have 120 seats (the total population divided by 30,000, the minimum ratio of representation specified in the Constitution).

To find out how many representatives Connecticut should have, they multiplied the ratio of the state's population to the total population by the size of the House to get the ideal quota:

$$\frac{236,841}{3,615,920} \cdot 120 \approx 7.860$$

So in the first round, Connecticut would be assigned 7 representatives.

1790 Census Results

State	Population	Ideal quota	Number of representatives (integer part)	Number of additional representatives (based on greatest remainder)	Total number of representatives based on Hamilton's method
Connecticut	236,841	7.860	7		
Delaware	55,540				
Georgia	70,835				
Kentucky	68,705				
Maryland	278,514				
Massachusetts	475,327				
New Hampshire	141,822				
New Jersey	179,570				
New York	331,589				
North Carolina	353,523				
Pennsylvania	432,879				
Rhode Island	68,446				
South Carolina	206,236				
Vermont	85,533				
Virginia	630,560				
	Total 3,615,920		Integer sum _____	Total number of additional representatives _____	Total number of representatives _____

Consider This . . .

1. In the 1790 census table, complete the column labeled "Ideal quota."

2. In the column labeled "Number of representatives (integer part)," record the integer part of each ideal quota. Find the sum of the entries in the column. Did this process fill all 120 seats in the House?

3. To fill the remaining seats (if there are any), find the state with the greatest remainder and give it one more representative. Continue allocating extra seats based on the descending order of the fractional part of the ideal quotas until you have filled the House.

4. Does this method seem like a fair way to apportion seats in the House? In which states do you think the citizens would be satisfied with this method?

Explore Further

Students in Broad County have been researching the historical background of apportionment in the process of setting up their student council, and they have decided to experiment with the methods proposed by early politicians in the United States. They are going to try Hamilton's method for apportionment. Assume that there will be 30 members on the newly formed student council.

5. Find the ideal quota for each school. To do this, multiply the ratio of the number of students in the school to the total student population by the number of student council members.

School	Student Population	Ideal quota	Number of representatives (integer part)	Additional representatives	Total number of representatives using Hamilton's method
Central City High	4464				
East High	3782				
West High	3284				
Hill High	1842				
Outland High	1288				
Sticks High	422				
	Total _____		Integer sum _____	Total number of additional representatives _____	Total number of representatives _____

6. The Constitution requires that each state have at least one representative. Similarly, the county school administration requires that each school have at least one representative. If there are any schools that have an ideal quota less than one, apportion them one representative.

7. Apportion the rest of the representatives using Hamilton's method.

8. Based on your apportionment using Hamilton's method, answer these questions.

• Does Hamilton's method seem like a fair method for apportioning the seats for the Broad County student council?

• How does Hamilton's method compare with the method you developed in Activity 9?

• Does Hamilton's method specifically benefit large or small schools?

9. The students decided to find out how the representatives to the Broad County student council would be apportioned when Wide High is allowed to join. Use Hamilton's method to find the new apportionment.

School	Student Population	Ideal quota	Number of representatives (integer part)	Additional representatives	Total number of representatives using Hamilton's method
Central City High	4464				
East High	3782				
West High	3284				
Wide High	2478				
Hill High	1842				
Outland High	1288				
Sticks High	422				
	Total _____		Integer sum _____	Additional representatives _____	Overall total _____

10. Which schools are most affected by the addition of Wide High?

11. Do you think that the students in each school will be satisfied with the results of this new apportionment?

Calculator Exploration

12. How will an apportionment be affected if you vary the number of seats to be assigned? This question can lead to some rather tedious computations without the aid of a calculator. You might want to try writing a calculator program that will automatically apportion the seats or use the one your teacher provides. Then you can more easily compare apportionments for different situations.

Research

13. Do some research to find out about the very first presidential veto.

14. Find out more about Alexander Hamilton. What other contributions did he make to U.S. history? Which state did he come from? What effect did this have on his politics?

15. What role does the census play in representation in the United States? Who is counted for apportionment purposes? How has this changed since 1790? How was the original census taken?

TEACHER'S NOTES

This activity introduces Alexander Hamilton's method for apportionment. In the original debate over apportionment, Hamilton's method was rejected in the end in favor of Jefferson's method. This was not because of any mathematical flaws, but because Jefferson argued that Hamilton's method did not meet the requirements of the Constitution. Jefferson believed that Hamilton's method could be used only with a House size of 120 and therefore might not be a good one to use as the country grew.

Hamilton's method does in fact have a flaw, which students explore in Activities 11 and 13. Student's will have varying opinions about whether or not the method is fair. Encourage them to discuss and even debate their opinions.

If it is feasible, encourage students to use programmable calculators or spreadsheets. Students will be using the same populations again in later activities; if they are using calculators, they may find it convenient to store lists in one calculator and then transfer lists as needed by linking to avoid having to re-enter a list each time it is needed. They will need to reserve two lists for the schools' populations—one with Wide High and one without.

If students came up with Hamilton's apportionment method in Activity 9, then some of the questions in this activity may be redundant. However, the questions may lead students toward a better definition of the method.

A calculator program for Hamilton's method is provided following Activity 18.

Answers

Consider This . . .

1–3.

State	Population	Ideal quota	Number of representatives (integer part)	Number of additional representatives (based on greatest remainder)	Total number of representatives based on Hamilton's method
Connecticut	236,841	7.860	7	1	8
Delaware	55,540	1.843	1	1	2
Georgia	70,835	2.351	2		2
Kentucky	68,705	2.280	2		2
Maryland	278,514	9.243	9		9
Massachusetts	475,327	15.774	15	1	16
New Hampshire	141,822	4.707	4	1	5
New Jersey	179,570	5.959	5	1	6
New York	331,589	11.004	11		11
North Carolina	353,523	11.732	11	1	12
Pennsylvania	432,879	14.366	14		14
Rhode Island	68,446	2.271	2		2
South Carolina	206,236	6.844	6	1	7
Vermont	85,533	2.839	2	1	3
Virginia	630,560	20.926	20	1	21
	Total 3,615,920		Integer sum 111	Total number of additional representatives 9	Total number of representatives 120

4. Answers will vary.

Explore Further

5–7. See Table.

School	Student Population	Ideal quota	Number of representatives (integer part)	Additional representatives	Total number of representatives using Hamilton's method
Central City High	4464	8.879	8	1	9
East High	3782	7.523	7		7
West High	3284	6.532	6		6
Hill High	1842	3.664	3	1	4
Outland High	1288	2.562	2	1	3
Sticks High	422	0.839	1		1
	Total 15,082		Integer sum 27	Additional representatives 3	Overall total 30

8. Answers will vary.

9.

School	Student Population	Ideal quota	Number of representatives (integer part)	Additional representatives	Total number of representatives using Hamilton's method
Central City High	4464	7.626	7	1	8
East High	3782	6.461	6		6
West High	3284	5.610	5	1	6
Wide High	2478	4.233	4		4
Hill High	1842	3.147	3		3
Outland High	1288	2.200	2		2
Sticks High	422	0.721	1		1
	Total 17,560		Integer sum 28	Additional representatives 2	Overall total 30

The sum of the student populations is 17,560. The ratio of representation will be 17,560/30 = 585.33 ≈ 585.

10. Central City High, East High, Hill High, and Outland High each lose one representative. The change in representation is spread evenly over large and small schools.

11. Answers will vary.

Calculator Exploration

12. If some of your students know how to program their calculator, let them write a program to compute results using Hamilton's method. Blackline masters for all of the calculator programs follow Activity 18.

Research

13. The first presidential veto occurred when George Washington vetoed the bill that would have made Hamilton's method the law for apportionment.

14. Alexander Hamilton lived from 1755 to 1804. He was the first U.S. Secretary of the Treasury. He led a very colorful life. He was born in the British West Indies to parents who were not married to each other at the time, and he died in a duel. In researching his life, students may enjoy reading about the role he played in the Revolutionary War and the creation of our government.

15. The U.S. Constitution specifies that an official census needs to be taken every ten years for the purpose of apportioning representatives. Taking the first census was quite an ordeal, and the methods varied from state to state. No attempt was made in the first census to include the populations in the northwest and southwest territories. Although an attempt was made to count all the inhabitants of the states, Native Americans were not included in the count for apportionment since they were not taxed and couldn't vote. For apportionment purposes, slaves were counted as three-fifths of a person.

THOMAS JEFFERSON'S METHOD OF APPORTIONMENT

The results of the first census were reported to the U.S. Congress in 1791, and the apportionment struggles began. The debate was heated. There were two opposing camps—Thomas Jefferson was the leader of a group of Republicans who were in conflict with the Federalist forces led by Hamilton. In the end, Hamilton's method was rejected, not because of mathematical flaws, but because Jefferson successfully argued that Hamilton's method did not meet the requirements of the Constitution. "But instead of such a *single* common ratio, or uniform divisor, as prescribed by the Constitution, the bill [Hamilton's method] has applied *two ratios*, at least to the different States . . . . And if *two* ratios be applied, then fifteen may, and the distribution becomes arbitrary . . ."[1]

Jefferson argued that his method could be used far into the future.

Jefferson's method was adopted by both houses of Congress and signed into law on April 14, 1792. The bill took only two days to pass the House, despite a last-ditch effort to increase the size of the House. According to this bill, each member of the House of Representatives would represent 33,000 people.

One of the reasons Jefferson preferred his method was because it offered a method for apportionment that was independent of the size of the House or the population of the country. In contrast, he believed that Hamilton's method applied only to an apportionment of 120 seats, without stating any rule for determining an apportionment that could be applied in future years. Jefferson's method was used until 1841 and is still in use in many countries, including Belgium, the Netherlands, Israel, Liechtenstein, Finland, Germany, Brazil, and Austria. It was reinvented by a Belgian lawyer named Victor d'Hondt in 1878 and is sometimes referred to as d'Hondt's method, the Hagenbach-Bischoff method, or the method of **highest averages** or **greatest divisors**.

Jefferson's method works this way.

*   First, choose the size of the House to be apportioned. (The size of the House of Representatives is determined by the existing House and Senate.)

*   Then find a value for x so that when the representative population of each state is divided by x, the whole numbers that result when you round *down* sum to the House size you want. Each state is assigned the whole number of representatives that results when its quotient is rounded down except, of course, those states whose value rounded down would be zero. In this case, assign the state one representative. The trick is to find a divisor that works.

    Eventually, Jefferson and his colleagues agreed that the House of Representatives should contain 105 members, using the divisor 33,000.

1790 Census Population

State	Population	Jefferson apportionment with 105 seats
Connecticut	236,841	
Delaware	55,540	
Georgia	70,835	
Kentucky	68,705	
Maryland	278,514	
Massachusetts	475,327	
New Hampshire	141,822	
New Jersey	179,570	
New York	331,589	
North Carolina	353,523	
Pennsylvania	432,879	
Rhode Island	68,446	
South Carolina	206,236	
Vermont	85,533	
Virginia	630,560	
Total	3,615,920	

To find the correct apportionment for each state, Jefferson found

$$\text{INT}\left(\frac{\text{population}}{33,000}\right).$$

(Remember that INT is the integer function. It means round down.) To find the

apportionment for Connecticut, find $\text{INT}\left(\dfrac{236,841}{33,000}\right)$. First divide 236,841 by 33,000, which gives 7.177. Then find INT(7.177) which is 7. So Connecticut would receive 7 representatives.

Consider This . . .

1. Use the 1790 census results to compute the original apportionment using Jefferson's method. (Note: Your calculator can perform the INT function for you. You can also use the list functions of your calculator or a spreadsheet.)

2. Find the sum of the numbers of representatives. Does it add to the original 105 members?

3. Was Jefferson's method more favorable to large or small states?

4. Which method do you prefer, Jefferson's or Hamilton's? Why?

5. Is 33,000 the greatest divisor that gives the apportionment above? Is there only one divisor that works, or is there a range of divisors that will give the same apportionment?

> The students at Central City High decide that they want to try Jefferson's method and compare it to the results of Hamilton's method. To use Jefferson's method, they have to find a divisor d so that when the population of each school is divided by d, and the integer values of these quotients are found, the sum of those values will give the desired number of students on the student council. (Remember, the administration wanted 30 students on the student council.)
>
> The students realized that they wanted to find a value of d so that
>
> $$\text{INT}\left(\frac{4464}{d}\right)+\text{INT}\left(\frac{3782}{d}\right)+\text{INT}\left(\frac{3284}{d}\right)+\text{INT}\left(\frac{1842}{d}\right)+\text{INT}\left(\frac{1288}{d}\right)+\text{INT}\left(\frac{422}{d}\right)=30.$$
>
> The first divisor they tried was 400. This worked out to
>
> $$\text{INT}\left(\frac{4464}{400}\right)+\text{INT}\left(\frac{3782}{400}\right)+\text{INT}\left(\frac{3284}{400}\right)+\text{INT}\left(\frac{1842}{400}\right)+\text{INT}\left(\frac{1288}{400}\right)+\text{INT}\left(\frac{422}{400}\right)=36.$$

The result using a divisor of 400 was too high, so next they tried a divisor of 422. They wanted to be sure that Sticks High had at least one representative.

$$\text{INT}\left(\frac{4464}{422}\right) + \text{INT}\left(\frac{3782}{422}\right) + \text{INT}\left(\frac{3284}{422}\right) + \text{INT}\left(\frac{1842}{422}\right) + \text{INT}\left(\frac{1288}{422}\right) + \text{INT}\left(\frac{422}{422}\right) = 33$$

The result using a divisor of 422 was still too low. Some of the other students remembered that according to the Constitution each state has to have at least one representative, so they suggested assigning a representative to any school that ends up with fewer than one representative. The students agreed to this plan and decided to try a larger divisor.

After several tries, they found that the divisor 469 gave them a student council with 30 seats if they assigned one representative to Sticks High.

Explore Further

6. Use the results with a divisor of 469 to complete the following table.

School	Student Population	Quotient	Jefferson apportionment with 30 seats
Central City High	4464		
East High	3782		
West High	3284		
Hill High	1842		
Outland High	1288		
Sticks High	422		

7. In which schools do you think the students will be most and least pleased by the results of Jefferson's method?

8. Compare the results using Jefferson's apportionment method to the results of the apportionment using Hamilton's method.

    •   Which method seems fairer?

    •   Which method do you prefer and why?

9. Use Jefferson's method to determine the apportionment when representatives for Wide High join the student council. Do this for a 30-member student council.

School	Student Population	Quotient (d =)	Jefferson apportionment with 30 seats
Central City High	4464		
East High	3782		
West High	3284		
Wide High	2478		
Hill High	1842		
Outland High	1288		
Sticks High	422		

Calculator Exploration

It didn't take the students long to realize what a nasty job apportionment must have been before the days of calculators and computers! If you have a programmable calculator, you might want to write a program to compute the apportionment using Jefferson's method. Or you can use the program your teacher provides.

10. Use the Jefferson program to find an apportionment for the student council with 32 seats. How does this apportionment compare to the apportionment you calculated in Question 6 with 30 seats? Are any of the schools better or less well represented? Which schools benefit from the larger council size?

School	Student Population	Quotient (d =)	Jefferson apportionment with 32 seats
Central City High	4464		
East High	3782		
West High	3284		
Hill High	1842		
Outland High	1288		
Sticks High	422		

11. Use the Jefferson program to apportion seats for a 32-seat student council for the next school year, when Wide High will join the student council.

School	Student Population	Quotient ($d =$)	Jefferson apportionment with 32 seats
Central City High	4464		
East High	3782		
West High	3284		
Wide High	2478		
Hill High	1842		
Outland High	1288		
Sticks High	422		

12. Experiment with different divisors and sizes of the student council until you find a size and apportionment that you would want to recommend to the other students and administration. Use the table below to record your results, and give some explanation of why you prefer the apportionment you have chosen.

School	Student Population	Quotient ($d =$)	Jefferson apportionment with ___ seats
Central City High	4464		
East High	3782		
West High	3284		
Wide High	2478		
Hill High	1842		
Outland High	1288		
Sticks High	422		

Research

13. Research the early Democrat Republicans and Federalists. What was each group interested in preserving?

14. Research Thomas Jefferson. What other contributions did he make to United States history?

TEACHER'S NOTES

Jefferson's method is the first of the "divisor" methods, which involve adjusting the divisor to make the apportionment work. For this method, Jefferson specified that one should find a divisor that gives the desired apportionment.

If possible, encourage your students to use calculators with list capabilities or a computer spreadsheet. If you don't have access to this technology, ask half your class to do Question 10 and the other half Question 11. The two groups can share their results with each other. Each student should complete Question 12 and develop his or her own apportionment.

A calculator program for Jefferson's method is provided following Activity 18.

Answers

Consider This . . .

1, 2.

State	Population	Jefferson apportionment with 105 seats
Connecticut	236,841	7
Delaware	55,540	1
Georgia	70,835	2
Kentucky	68,705	2
Maryland	278,514	8
Massachusetts	475,327	14
New Hampshire	141,822	4
New Jersey	179,570	5
New York	331,589	10
North Carolina	353,523	10
Pennsylvania	432,879	13
Rhode Island	68,446	2
South Carolina	206,236	6
Vermont	85,533	2
Virginia	630,560	19
Total	3,615,920	105

3. Answers will vary. History has shown that Jefferson's method tends to favor larger states. Students will explore this further in later activities.

4. Answers will vary.

5. The range of divisors that work is 32,139–33,158.

Explore Further

6.

School	Student Population	Quotient	Jefferson apportionment with 30 seats
Central City High	4464	9.518	9
East High	3782	8.064	8
West High	3284	7.002	7
Hill High	1842	3.928	3
Outland High	1288	2.746	2
Sticks High	422	.09	1

7. Answers will vary.

8.

School	Hamilton apportionment	Jefferson apportionment with 30 seats
Central City High	9	9
East High	7	8
West High	6	7
Hill High	4	3
Outland High	3	2
Sticks High	1	1

There may be varying opinions as to which method is fairer. Encourage students to discuss this. Activity 13 has more discussion on the fairness of the methods, and criteria will be developed. Encourage students to come up with their own criteria for fairness now.

9. The range of divisors that work is 541–547.

School	Student Population	Quotient	Jefferson apportionment with 30 seats
Central City High	4464	8.161	8
East High	3782	6.914	6
West High	3284	6.004	6
Wide High	2478	4.53	4
Hill High	1842	3.367	3
Outland High	1288	2.355	2
Sticks High	422	0.771	1

Calculator Exploration

10. The range of divisors that work is 430–446.

School	Student Population	Quotient	Jefferson apportionment with 32 seats
Central City High	4464	10.262	10
East High	3782	8.6943	8
West High	3284	7.5494	7
Hill High	1842	4.2345	4
Outland High	1288	2.9609	2
Sticks High	422	0.97011	1

The largest school and a midsize school each gained a representative.

11. The only divisor that works is 496.

School	Student Population	Quotient	Jefferson apportionment with 32 seats
Central City High	4464	9	9
East High	3782	7.625	7
West High	3284	6.621	6
Wide High	2478	4.996	4
Hill High	1842	3.7137	3
Outland High	1288	2.5958	2
Sticks High	422	0.85051	1

12. Answers will vary.

Research

13. Hamilton and Jefferson were the leaders of the first two political parties in the United States. At first, the hope had been to establish a government of superior persons who would be above party, but Hamilton and Jefferson soon found that they needed supporters of their policies. In foreign affairs, Hamilton and the Federalists wanted to keep close ties with England. Jefferson and the Democrat Republicans were more in favor of strengthening the old attachment to France. Hamilton and Jefferson feuded from 1791 to 1793, attempting to drive each other out of the cabinet. They used party newspapers to attack each other and their policies, and each tried to turn President Washington against the other.

14. Thomas Jefferson lived from 1743 to 1826. He was the third president of the United States, a principal author of the Declaration of Independence, and an extremely influential political philosopher.

Reference Note

1. Thomas Jefferson. "Opinion on the Bill Apportioning Representation." In *The Works of Thomas Jefferson*, ed. Paul Leicester Ford (New York and London: G. P. Putnam's Sons, 1904), 6: 463–464.

DANIEL WEBSTER'S METHOD OF APPORTIONMENT

Jefferson's method was used to apportion the House of Representatives from 1792 to 1841, but by the 1830s politicians were once again struggling over the issue of apportionment. John Quincy Adams, at the time a representative from Massachusetts and a former president, wrote in his memoirs:

> I passed an entirely sleepless night. The iniquity of the Apportionment bill, and the disreputable means by which so partial and unjust a distribution of the representation had been effected, agitated me so that I could not close my eyes.[1]

Thank goodness Daniel Webster and the founders were not proficient at calculus.

Mr. Adams was referring to a bill authored by James K. Polk of Tennessee, which used Jefferson's method of apportionment with an increased divisor of 47,700. Polk's bill improved the representation of several key states but hurt the representation of some of the earliest New England states.

The problem stemmed from the growth in the U.S. population. The country had grown from 15 states and a census population of 3,615,920 in 1790 to a census population of 12,866,020 in 24 states in 1830. The size of the House of Representatives had steadily increased to 240 members, and the divisor had changed only from 33,000 to 47,700.

There was a flurry of discussion about apportionment, and many new methods were proposed and discarded as unfair. Historical evidence showed that Jefferson's method favored the larger states. Many people and politicians thought it was time for a new method to be developed.

The method that emerged was developed by Daniel Webster in 1832. Webster referred to the Constitution and to the arguments of Washington, Hamilton, and Jefferson from the first discussion of apportionment. He also received advice from mathematicians around the country and in the end proposed this method:

> Let the rule be that the population of each State be divided by a common divisor, and, in addition to the number of members resulting from such division, a member shall be allowed to each State whose fraction exceeds a moiety of the divisor.[2]

Webster's method is similar to Jefferson's method in that a divisor that provides the desired House size must be selected. But instead of always rounding down, as in Jefferson's method, the fractions are rounded according to the standard convention—down for fractions less than 0.5, and up for fractions of 0.5 and above.

The following table shows the population of nine selected states in 1830.

State	Population	Quotient (population/49,800)	Apportionment
New York	1,918,578	38.526	39
Pennsylvania	1,348,072		
Kentucky	621,832		
Vermont	280,657		
Louisiana	171,904		
Illinois	157,147		
Missouri	130,491		
Mississippi	110,358		
Delaware	75,432		
Total population	11,931,000		

Webster first proposed using this method with a divisor of 49,800. To find the apportionment for New York, he divided 1,918,578 by 49,800 to get 38.526, which is then rounded to 39.

Consider This . . .

1. Based on the populations listed in the table, apportion the states' representatives using Webster's method.

2. Does this method seem fair? Does it seem to favor large or small states?

3. Which method do you prefer: Jefferson's, Hamilton's or Webster's? Why?

4. It may seem difficult to express Webster's method in a formula, but there is a slight trick to it. Round each number in a–d using the standard convention.

   a. 3.124   b. 4.00   c. 5.523   d. 8.99

   Now for each result, n, find INT($n + 0.5$). What do you notice?

   The students at Central City High have decided to give Webster's method a try. They realize that they want to find a divisor d so that when the population of each school is divided by d and the resulting quotient is rounded, the sum of all the rounded quotients will equal 30. They realize that they could write this as the equation

   $$\text{INT}\left(\frac{4464}{d} + 0.5\right) + \text{INT}\left(\frac{3782}{d} + 0.5\right) + \text{INT}\left(\frac{3284}{d} + 0.5\right) + \text{INT}\left(\frac{1842}{d} + 0.5\right) + \text{INT}\left(\frac{1288}{d} + 0.5\right) + \text{INT}\left(\frac{422}{d} + 0.5\right) = 30.$$

   Some of the students decided to start with the divisor 469, which worked for Jefferson's method.

School	Student Population	Webster apportionment with 30 seats ($d = 469$)
Central City High	4464	10
East High	3782	8
West High	3284	7
Hill High	1842	4
Outland High	1288	3
Sticks High	422	1
Total		33

   A total of 33 is too large. What divisor would you try next? (You may find it useful to use the list function in your calculator or a computer spreadsheet!)

5. Find a divisor that will satisfy the equation above for the student council apportionment.

6. Complete the table below, showing the apportionment that results using Webster's method.

School	Student Population	Webster apportionment with 30 seats
Central City High	4464	
East High	3782	
West High	3284	
Hill High	1842	
Outland High	1288	
Sticks High	422	

Explore Further

7. Use Webster's method to apportion seats for the student council with 32 seats. How does this apportionment compare to the apportionment you calculated above with 30 seats? Are any of the schools better or less well represented? Which schools benefit from the larger council size?

School	Student Population	Webster apportionment for 32 seats
Central City High	4464	
East High	3782	
West High	3284	
Hill High	1842	
Outland High	1288	
Sticks High	422	

8. Use Webster's method to apportion seats for the student council with 30 seats when Wide High joins the council.

School	Student Population	Webster apportionment with 30 seats
Central City High	4464	
East High	3782	
West High	3284	
Wide High	2478	
Hill High	1842	
Outland High	1288	
Sticks High	422	

The Method of John Quincy Adams

Choose the size of the house to be apportioned. Find a divisor d so that the smallest whole numbers containing the quotients of the states sum to the required total. Give to each state its whole number.

9. John Quincy Adams also proposed a method for apportionment that is similar to Jefferson's method except that the quotients are always rounded up. Experiment with his method using the data from Broad County.

School	Student Population	Adams apportionment for 30 seats ($d =$)	Adams apportionment for 32 seats ($d =$)
Central City High	4464		
East High	3782		
West High	3284		
Hill High	1842		
Outland High	1288		
Sticks High	422		

School	Student Population	Adams apportionment for 30 seats ($d =$)	Adams apportionment for 32 seats ($d =$)
Central City High	4464		
East High	3782		
West High	3284		
Wide High	2478		
Hill High	1842		
Outland High	1288		
Sticks High	422		

10. Does Adams's method favor large or small populations?

Calculator Exploration

11. The students at Central City High soon realized that Webster's method, like Jefferson's method, was perfect for their programmable calculators. Write your own program or use the program provided by your teacher.

12. Use Webster's method to create your own apportionment of the student council. Experiment with different divisors and sizes of the council until you find a size and apportionment you would want to recommend to the other students and the administration. Use the table below to present your results, and give some explanation of why you prefer the apportionment you have chosen.

School	Student Population	Webster apportionment with ___ seats
Central City High	4464	
East High	3782	
West High	3284	
Wide High	2478	
Hill High	1842	
Outland High	1288	
Sticks High	422	

13. Adams's method is also easy to use with a programmable calculator. Create a program of your own or use the program your teacher provides to create your own apportionment of the student council. Experiment with different divisors and sizes of the council until you find a size and apportionment you would want to recommend to the other students and the administration. Use the table below to present your results, and give some explanation of why you prefer the apportionment you have chosen.

School	Student Population	Adams apportionment with ___ seats
Central City High	4464	
East High	3782	
West High	3284	
Wide High	2478	
Hill High	1842	
Outland High	1288	
Sticks High	422	

Research

14. By the year 1832, Daniel Webster was regarded by many people as the greatest man in America, although others called him Black Dan. Do some research to discover more about him.

15. Do some research and learn about John Quincy Adams. What contributions did he make to early American history?

TEACHER'S NOTES

In this activity, students explore the apportionment method of Daniel Webster. His method seems the most intuitively fair of the divisor methods, since it involves rounding in the conventional way.

Questions 9 and 10 investigate the method of John Quincy Adams. These questions can be used as an extension of the activity, or they can be skipped.

Encourage students to use calculators for this activity. Many calculators have a round function that will round numbers according to the standard convention. If students are working with programmable calculators or a calculator spreadsheet, they can input the populations in one list, compute the quotient in a second, round it in a third, and then use the calculator or spreadsheet functions to find the sum of this last list. It is truly amazing that early politicians computed these apportionments without the aid of calculators and computers. We have to admire their perseverance.

Calculator programs for Webster's method and Adams's method are provided following Activity 18.

Answers

Consider This . . .

1.

State	Population	Quotient (population/49,800)	Apportionment
New York	1,918,578	38.526	39
Pennsylvania	1,348,072	27.07	27
Kentucky	621,832	12.487	12
Vermont	280,657	5.636	6
Louisiana	171,904	3.452	3
Illinois	157,147	3.156	3
Missouri	130,491	2.619	3
Mississippi	110,358	2.216	2
Delaware	75,432	1.5157	2
Total population	11,931,000		

2. Students will have their own opinions as to which method is fairest.

3. Answers will vary.

4. a. 3　　b. 4　　c. 6　　d. 9

In Question 4, students discover that the formula INT(n + 0.5) gives the value of n rounded by standard convention. Some calculators also have a round function.

5. Any divisor between 506 and 515 works.

6.

School	Student Population	Webster apportionment with 30 seats
Central City High	4464	9
East High	3782	7
West High	3284	6
Hill High	1842	4
Outland High	1288	3
Sticks High	422	1

If students have a list function on their calculators, they can simplify their work by entering the populations into one of the lists and performing the calculations in another list.

Explore Further

7. To apportion a council with 32 seats, use a divisor of 471. East High and West High each gain one seat.

School	Student Population	Webster apportionment for 32 seats
Central City High	4464	9
East High	3782	7
West High	3284	6
Hill High	1842	4
Outland High	1288	3
Sticks High	422	1

8. A divisor of 585 gives the following apportionment:

School	Student Population	Webster apportionment with 30 seats
Central City High	4464	8
East High	3782	6
West High	3284	6
Wide High	2478	4
Hill High	1842	3
Outland High	1288	2
Sticks High	422	1

9. The range of divisors is given for each apportionment.

School	Student Population	Adams apportionment for 30 seats (548 - 557)	Adams apportionment for 32 seats (496 - 540)
Central City High	4464	9	9
East High	3782	7	8
West High	3284	6	7
Hill High	1842	4	4
Outland High	1288	3	3
Sticks High	422	1	1

School	Student Population	Adams apportionment for 30 seats (638 - 643)	Adams apportionment for 32 seats (620 - 630)
Central City High	4464	7	8
East High	3782	6	7
West High	3284	6	6
Wide High	2478	4	4
Hill High	1842	3	3
Outland High	1288	3	3
Sticks High	422	1	1

10. Adams's method for apportionment favors small populations.

Calculator Exploration

11. The program is on a blackline master following Activity 18.

12. Answers will vary.

13. Answers will vary.

Research

14. Daniel was one of the most prominent politicians of his time and a brilliant orator. He was the foremost advocate of American nationalism of his era. He served in the House and in the Senate and became Secretary of State in July 1850 under President Millard Fillmore. He was "Black Dan" to those who saw him as a compromiser on matters of principle, for example, his willingness to compromise on the issue of slavery in order to preserve the Union. His personal life also contributed to his "Black Dan" image. He lived extravagantly, was always in debt, and was saved from bankruptcy by wealthy New England supporters who paid his bills.

15. John Quincy Adams was the sixth president of the United States. He served in the Massachusetts Senate as well as the U.S. Senate. He was also the American ambassador to Holland, Prussia, and Russia. He served as Secretary of State under James Monroe. After his presidential term, he returned to the House of Representatives where he served for nine consecutive terms. Adams died on February 23, 1848; he was the last surviving statesman of the American Revolution.

Reference Notes

1. John Quincy Adams. *The Memoirs of John Quincy Adams*, ed. Charles Francis Adams (Philadelphia: J. B. Lipponcott & Co., 1876), 8:474.

2. Daniel Webster. *The Writings and Speeches of Daniel Webster*, National Edition (Boston: Little, Brown & Co., 1903), 6:120.

IS IT FAIR?

How do you decide whether a method for apportioning representatives is fair? In the last few activities, you examined the methods of Hamilton, Jefferson, Webster, and Adams. You used each method to apportion seats for the Broad County student council, and in each activity you were asked if you thought the method was fair. Which method do you prefer? Which method do you think is fairest? How do you decide?

"All I did was ask it to calculate a fair apportionment method."

These questions have plagued politicians as they have tried to determine which apportionment method to use. Daniel Webster pointed out that no method can apportion representatives precisely and perfectly. However, he also maintained that whether a method was fair or not was not just a matter of opinion, but a mathematical certainty.

One of the first measures used by Hamilton's followers to judge fairness was the "Rule of Three." It was called this because three quantities are involved: the total population, a state's population, and the number of representatives to be apportioned. The **ideal quota** for each state is found by dividing the state's population by the total population and then multiplying by the total number of representatives to be apportioned. When you use Hamilton's method for apportionment, you calculate each state's ideal quota, which will stay constant for any given House size, regardless of the apportionment method you use. This ideal quota is different from the quantity you get when you divide a state's population by the particular divisor you are using in an apportionment method, which is what makes the divisor methods different from Hamilton's method.

Once you have found the quota for each state, compare the apportionment for each state to its quota. If a method *satisfies quota*, each state will get at least as many representatives as its ideal quota rounded down and no more representatives than its ideal quota rounded up. For example, if a state's ideal quota is 13.459, then it should receive no fewer than 13 representatives and no more than 14 representatives. If this state receives fewer than 13 representatives or more than 14 representatives, then the apportionment method used *violates quota*. Some methods never violate quota, while others occasionally will.

The students of Central City High decided that it was time for a field trip to research the problem of finding a fair method of apportionment to the student council. They planned a trip to their sister school in Dale County, which had just set up a student council. The students at Valley High were eager to share their data.

Dale County Student Population by School

School	Student population
North High	9061
South High	7179
Valley High	5259
Meadow High	3319
Ridge High	1182
Total	26,000

Consider This . . .

1. Compute the ratio of representation for each council size in the table below. To do this, divide each population by the number of seats.

Number of seats	26	27	40
Ratio of representation			

2. Compute the ideal quotas for each council size in the table below. To do this, divide each population by the total population (26,000) and multiply by the number of members on the council.

School	Ideal quota for 26 seats	Ideal quota for 27 seats	Ideal quota for 40 seats
North High	9.061	9.4095	13.94
South High	7.179	7.4551	11.045
Valley High	5.259	5.4613	8.0908
Meadow High	3.319	3.4467	5.1062
Ridge High	1.182	1.2275	1.8185

School	26 seats	27 seats	40 seats
North High			
South High			
Valley High			
Meadow High			
Ridge High			

3. Use Hamilton's method to calculate the number of representatives each school will have in a student council with 26 seats, 27 seats, and 40 seats.

4. Does it appear that Hamilton's method satisfies quota? Will Hamilton's method always satisfy quota? Why or why not?

5. Do you think that the students of Meadow High will be satisfied with the apportionment of 27 seats? Why or why not?

6. The problem faced by Meadow High when the size of the council was increased from 26 to 27 is called the Alabama paradox. Explain this paradox in your own words.

7. If the student council size remains fixed at 26 seats as the school district grows, will the apportionment change as the number of students increases? Assume that the proportion of students at each school remains constant.

Explore Further

8. Use Jefferson's method to apportion seats for the Dale County student council.

Apportionment Using Jefferson's Method

School	26 seats ($d = ?$)	27 seats ($d = ?$)	40 seats ($d = ?$)
North High			
South High			
Valley High			
Meadow High			
Ridge High			

- Does Jefferson's apportionment appear to satisfy quota?

- Do these results seem to be fair? Do any problems arise from the increase in size of the student council?

- If the student council size remains fixed at 26 seats as the school district grows, will the apportionment change as the number of students increases? Assume that the proportion of students at each school remains constant.

9. Use Webster's method to apportion seats for the Dale county student council.

Apportionment Using Webster's Method

School	26 seats ($d=?$)	27 seats ($d=?$)	40 seats ($d=?$)
North High			
South High			
Valley High			
Meadow High			
Ridge High			

- Does Webster's apportionment appear to satisfy quota?

- Do these results seem to be fair? Do any problems arise from the increase in size of the student council?

- If the student council size remains fixed at 26 seats as the school district grows, will the apportionment change as the number of students increases? Assume that the proportion of students at each school remains constant.

10. Use Adams's method to apportion seats for the Dale County student council.

Apportionment Using Adams's Method

School	26 seats ($d=?$)	27 seats ($d=?$)	40 seats ($d=?$)
North High			
South High			
Valley High			
Meadow High			
Ridge High			

- Does Adams's apportionment appear to satisfy quota?

- Do these results seem to be fair? Do any problems arise from the increase in size of the student council?

- If the student council size remains fixed at 26 seats as the school district grows, will the apportionment change as the number of students increases? Assume that the proportion of students at each school remains constant.

Calculator Exploration

11. The students at Central City High have also been trying to collect information on the Internet to help them make their decision on how to apportion the student council. They found some interesting information from the Four Corners Water District. Use Webster's method and your calculator to apportion seats for the 35-seat water board in Four Corners Water District.

County	Population	Number of representatives ($d = ?$)	Ideal quota
South East County (SE)	70,653		
North West County (NW)	117,404		
North East County (NE)	210,923		
South West County (SW)	1,194,456		
Total	1,593,436		

- Compute the ideal quota for each part of the county. Does Webster's method satisfy quota in this case?

- Does this seem like a fair apportionment to you? Why or why not?

TEACHER'S NOTES

This activity explores some criteria for fairness, namely, quota and the Alabama paradox. Students will learn more about the Alabama paradox and other paradoxes in Activity 14. Be sure students understand what the term "paradox" means.
This activity can be used in several ways.

- You can let students compute the apportionments using the methods from the three previous activities. By using the four methods in the same activity, students will become more comfortable with them, and will be better able to compare and contrast them. If students are using calculator programs, finding the apportionments will not be too time-consuming.

- If the mathematics of computing the apportionments is overwhelming for your students, you can provide the divisors for each apportionment. Write the divisors on the master before you copy the activity so that each student will have them on hand.

- Another alternative is to provide the students with a copy of the blackline master following this activity. This master contains all the apportionments necessary to complete the activity.

Consider This . . .

1.

Number of seats	26	27	40
Ratio of representation	1000:1	963:1	650:1

2.

School	Ideal quota for 26 seats	Ideal quota for 27 seats	Ideal quota for 40 seats
North High	9.061	9.4095	13.94
South High	7.179	7.4551	11.045
Valley High	5.259	5.4613	8.0908
Meadow High	3.319	3.4467	5.1062
Ridge High	1.182	1.2275	1.8185

If students have calculators with a list function, then this calculation is fairly simple. Enter the school populations in one list, and in another list divide the first list by 26,000. To get the quota, you can multiply the entries in the second list by the required council sizes.

3. Apportionment Using Hamilton's Method

School	26 seats	27 seats	40 seats
North High	9	9	14
South High	7	8	11
Valley High	5	6	8
Meadow High	4	3	5
Ridge High	1	1	2

4. Hamilton's method satisfies quota for all student council sizes. It will, in fact, always satisfy quota.

5. Students at Meadow High may feel that for 27 seats the method is unfair. Though the student council has increased in size and there have been no changes in the population, Meadow High has lost a seat.

6. The Alabama paradox arises when the size of the House increases and this increase in size causes a state to lose a seat. It is discussed in more detail in Activity 14. Encourage your students to explore further and discover how this could happen.

7. Hamilton's method is not affected by a rise in representative population. This property of Hamilton's method can be proved as follows:

> **Proof:** Suppose the ideal quota for each state is $\frac{x_i}{x} s$ where x_i is the population in each state, x is the total population, and s is the number of seats. If the population increases or decreases by a factor k, then the new total population is kx. If the relative proportion of the population for each state remains constant, then the new population of each state is given by $\frac{x_i}{x} \cdot kx = kx_i$. Therefore, the new ideal quota $\frac{kx_i}{kx} s = \frac{x_i}{x} s$, which is the same as the original ideal quota.

Explore Further

8. Apportionment Using Jefferson's Method

School	26 seats ($d = 906$)	27 seats ($d = 897$)	40 seats ($d = 600$)
North High	10	10	15
South High	7	8	11
Valley High	5	5	8
Meadow High	3	3	5
Ridge High	1	1	1

- Jefferson's method doesn't satisfy quota for a council of 40 seats. The number of representatives for North High should be either 13 or 14.

- Answers will vary. It doesn't appear that Jefferson's method has a problem such as the Alabama paradox.

- The apportionment stays the same as the population increases. This can be proved as follows:

Proof: Consider the equation (1) $\sum \text{INT} \frac{x_i}{d_1} = s$ where x_i is the population in the ith state and d is a divisor that gives the required House size of s seats. Suppose the total population changes to kx; then the population in the ith state changes to kx_i. Therefore, you need to find a divisor d_2 so that $\sum \text{INT}\, k\, \frac{x_i}{d_1} = s$, but a comparison of this equation with equation (1) above shows that d_2 must be equal to kd_1. Therefore, the allotment for each state remains constant, namely, $\text{INT}\, \frac{x_i}{d_1}$.

9. Apportionment Using Webster's Method

School	26 seats ($d = 957$)	27 seats ($d = 956$)	40 seats ($d = 671$)
North High	9	9	14
South High	8	8	11
Valley High	5	6	8
Meadow High	3	3	5
Ridge High	1	1	2

- In this example, Webster's method does appear to satisfy quota. In a later problem, students will discover that Webster's method doesn't always satisfy quota.

- It appears that Webster's method is fair. There are no problems associated with increased council size.

- The Webster apportionment will stay the same as the population grows. The proof is similar to the proof for the Jefferson apportionment.

10. Apportionment Using Adams's Method

School	26 seats ($d = 1110$)	27 seats ($d = 1100$)	40 seats ($d = 690$)
North High	9	9	14
South High	7	7	11
Valley High	5	5	8
Meadow High	3	4	5
Ridge High	2	2	2

- Adams's method appears to satisfy quota, but there are cases where it does not.

- Answers will vary. Adams's method is not subject to the Alabama paradox.

* The apportionment will remain constant.

Calculator Exploration

11.

County	Population	Number of representatives ($d = 46{,}850$)	Ideal quota
South East County (SE)	70,653	2	1.5519
North West County (NW)	117,404	3	2.5788
North East County (NE)	210,923	5	4.6329
South West County (SW)	1,194,456	25	26.236
Total	1,593,436	35	

* No, it does not satisfy quota. South West County has fewer representatives than its ideal quota rounded down.

* Answers will vary.

Apportionments for Activity 13

1. Ratio of representation

Number of seats	26	27	40
Ratio of representation	1000:1	963:1	650:1

2. Ideal quota

School	Ideal quota for 26 seats	Ideal quota for 27 seats	Ideal quota for 40 seats
North High	9.061	9.4095	13.94
South High	7.179	7.4551	11.045
Valley High	5.259	5.4613	8.0908
Meadow High	3.319	3.4467	5.1062
Ridge High	1.182	1.2275	1.8185

3. Apportionment using Hamilton's method

School	26 seats	27 seats	40 seats
North High	9	9	14
South High	7	8	11
Valley High	5	6	8
Meadow High	4	3	5
Ridge High	1	1	2

8. Apportionment using Jefferson's method

School	26 seats ($d = 906$)	27 seats ($d = 897$)	40 seats ($d = 600$)
North High	10	10	15
South High	7	8	11
Valley High	5	5	8
Meadow High	3	3	5
Ridge High	1	1	1

9. Apportionment using Webster's method

School	26 seats ($d = 957$)	27 seats ($d = 956$)	40 seats ($d = 671$)
North High	9	9	14
South High	8	8	11
Valley High	5	6	8
Meadow High	3	3	5
Ridge High	1	1	2

10. Apportionment using Adams's method

School	26 seats ($d = 1110$)	27 seats ($d = 1100$)	40 seats ($d = 690$)
North High	9	9	14
South High	7	7	11
Valley High	5	5	8
Meadow High	3	4	5
Ridge High	2	2	2

11. Apportionment using Webster's method

County	Population	Number of representatives ($d = 46,850$)	Ideal quota
South East County (SE)	70,653	2	1.5519
North West County (NW)	117,404	3	2.5788
North East County (NE)	210,923	5	4.6329
South West County (SW)	1,194,456	25	26.236
Total	1,593,436	35	

PARADOXES OF APPORTIONMENT

In Activity 13, you discovered that there are problems with the apportionment methods you have explored so far. One of these problems is the failure to satisfy quota, and another is the Alabama paradox.

Following the 1850 census, Hamilton's apportionment method was enacted. It is usually referred to as Vinton's Method of 1850. The Alabama paradox was first identified after the 1870 census. With 270 members in the House, the state of Rhode Island was allotted two members under Hamilton's method, but when the House size was increased to 280, Rhode Island was given only one seat. Following the 1880

Congress did not react to the increasing problems of apportionment until C. W. Seaton discovered the "Alabama paradox."

census, C. W. Seaton, the chief clerk of the United States Census Office, computed apportionments using Hamilton's method for all sizes for the House of Representatives between 275 and 350 members. Seaton wrote a letter to Congress showing how Alabama was allotted eight representatives with a House size of 299 but only seven representatives when the House size was changed to 300. Finally, a House size of 325 was chosen because for that number Webster's and Hamilton's methods yielded the same results. After the 1900 census, compromise was no longer possible. Maine and Colorado, among other states, were affected by the Alabama paradox. In 1901, three decades after the Alabama paradox was first noticed, Hamilton's method was finally abandoned in favor of Webster's method. Congress seemed to be able to tolerate an occasional violation of quota, but it could not accept a method that allowed for the Alabama paradox.

In all the examples you explored in Activity 13, you found that Hamilton's method satisfied quota. In fact, Hamilton's method will always satisfy quota, but, as you discovered, it is subject to the Alabama paradox. You encountered this problem when you increased the size of the student council from 26 to 27 seats. The total number of students didn't change, the proportion of students in Meadow High didn't change, but Meadow High got fewer seats on a larger council.

You also discovered that Jefferson's and Webster's methods occasionally fail to satisfy quota. However, they do not seem to be subject to the Alabama paradox.

Consider This . . .

1. Create a convincing argument that divisor methods such as Jefferson's and Webster's avoid the Alabama paradox. It might be helpful to consider what happens to the divisor, d, and the quotient of each state (the representative population divided by d) as the size of the Congress increases.

2. In 1901, when the U.S. Congress rejected Hamilton's apportionment method and adopted Webster's method, it set a precedent that methods allowing the Alabama paradox cannot be used for apportionment. However, Congress was willing to let a method that might violate quota be used. Why do you think they would allow this?

It turns out that there are other paradoxes of apportionment. One, called the **population paradox**, occurs when changes in apportionment do not accurately reflect changes in population. This happened with Hamilton's method between 1900 and 1901. Virginia was growing much faster than Maine. The population of Virginia increased by 19,767 while Maine's population increased by 4648. Furthermore, Virginia's rate of growth relative to Maine's was almost 60% greater. However, even though Virginia became proportionally larger than Maine, Hamilton's method resulted in taking a seat from Virginia and giving it to Maine.

Yet another paradox, called the **new states paradox**, occurs with Hamilton's method. This paradox appeared when Oklahoma became a state in 1907. Oklahoma was entitled to about five seats in the House, but when these five seats were added and the total number of seats was reapportioned using Hamilton's method, New York would have had to give up a seat to Maine, even though there was no change in the population of Maine, New York, or any other state! This paradox can also occur when a state secedes from the Union.

You may be wondering if there is any method that avoids these paradoxes and satisfies quota. The answer is that no divisor method satisfies quota, in part because forcing all states to stay within quota does not affect large states in the same way it does small states. A difference of one seat has less effect on a larger state's proportion of representation than that of a smaller state.

Since there was no perfect method available, Webster's method was adopted as a compromise.

Historical evidence has since shown that Webster's method is the least likely to violate quota, and mathematics demonstrates that Webster's method is the one and only divisor method that stays near the quota.

3. Your group is the apportionment committee for one of the departments of SuperTec, a factory specializing in computer products for use in schools. SuperTec is owned by its employees. Each employee owns an equal share in the company and therefore must be equally represented in the leadership of the company. SuperTec is made up of four departments: production, development, sales, and service. Each department elects representatives to the board of trustees.

Department	Number of Employees	Apportionment
Development	241	
Production	673	
Sales	368	
Service	173	

Formulate a proposal for the apportionment of SuperTec's board of trustees. Use the questions below as a guide when you are formulating your proposal.

- How big should the board of trustees be? Why?

- Which apportionment method do you recommend using? Why? Are you going to require that your method satisfy quota? Are you willing to tolerate paradoxes?

- How should the addition of new departments be handled?

- How should growth in department populations be handled?

4. Compare your department's proposed apportionment to those of other departments. Can all the departments agree on a method of apportionment?

Explore Further

5. Apportionment is used in many applications other than politics. The Central City youth club offers five art classes each semester that are taught by the same teacher. In the preregistration for the classes, 51 students signed up for painting, 30 for sculpture, and 19 for lapidary. The table below shows the apportionment of the classes using Hamilton's method.

Course	Number of students	Ideal quota	Apportionment	Course average
Painting	51	2.55	3	17
Sculpture	30	1.50	1	19
Lapidary	19	0.95	1	19

When the courses began, the actual enrollments in the three classes changed to 52 students in painting, 33 in sculpture, and 15 in lapidary. The table below shows the new apportionment using Hamilton's method.

Course	Number of students	Ideal quota	Apportionment	Course average
Painting	52	2.60	2	26
Sculpture	33	1.65	2	16.5
Lapidary	15	0.75	1	15

Compare and analyze the results of the two apportionments and describe in your own words the problem that occurs with the change in enrollment. How serious a problem do you think this is?

6. Cygnet College is a small college with three divisions. Each division has the enrollment shown in the table below.

Division	Enrollment
Arts	690
Science	435
Business	375
Total	1500

- How would you apportion the five seats in the student senate to the three divisions?

- If the student numbers changed to 555, 465, and 480 next year, how would you apportion the five seats?

- Will any division gain students but lose representation due to the change in population?

Research

7. In the election of 1876, Rutherford B. Hayes was elected president. What role did the electoral college play in his election? How do you think this affected discussions about apportionment?

8. Sometimes the paradoxes discussed in this activity are referred to as the failure to satisfy **house monotonicity** or **quota monotonicity**. In a dictionary, find a definition for monotone that you think applies to this situation. Research what is meant by house monotonicity or quota monotonicity.

TEACHER'S NOTES

In this activity, students continue their exploration of the undesirable properties of the apportionment methods they have studied. Balinski and Young proved in the 1970s that any possible apportionment method, whether known or not yet discovered, must in fact produce some unpleasant result in some instances. This is an example of an impossibility theorem.

For the Consider This section of this activity, divide the class into groups representing the four departments of SuperTec. If you have enough students, you might want to have two groups represent each department. After each group has formulated a proposal, have the groups present their proposals to the class. Hold a class discussion in which the class, representing the employees of the plant, agrees on an apportionment method.

Answers

Consider This . . .

1. Divisor methods avoid the Alabama paradox because as the House size increases, the divisor, d, must be made smaller. As the divisor decreases, the quotient of each state (the representative population of the state divided by the divisor) increases. Each time this quotient passes an integer value in Jefferson's method or a specific decimal value in Webster's method, its state gets one more seat. Since no state's quotient can possibly get smaller, no state will ever lose a seat.

2. Congress found the possibility of paradoxes occurring more disturbing than an occasional violation of quota.

3. Answers will vary.

4. Answers will vary.

Explore Further

5. Answers will vary. The problem here is that the quota increased for painting, but its apportionment decreased. The situation in this problem illustrates the failure of **quota monotonicity**, which is referred to in Question 8. This is a problem in any reasonable apportionment method. It occurs when a group's quota increases but its apportionment decreases. This situation is different from the Alabama paradox, which is sometimes referred to as the failure of house monotonicity.

6. The tables show the apportionments for both populations.

Division	Enrollment	Hamilton	Jefferson	Webster	Adams
Arts	690	2	3	2	2
Science	435	2	1	2	2
Business	375	1	1	1	1
Total	1500				

Division	Enrollment	Hamilton	Jefferson	Webster	Adams
Arts	555	2	2	2	2
Science	465	1	1	1	1
Business	480	2	2	2	2
Total	1500				

Each method except Jefferson's results in the science division losing a seat even though its size has increased. Students may have varying opinions as to the fairness of this.

Research

7. In the 1876 presidential election, Samuel J. Tilden received 4,300,590 popular votes to Rutherford B. Hayes's 4,036,298 votes. But the electoral college, which is influenced by the apportionment of the House, elected Hayes.

8. A set of values is monotonic if the values in the set increase or decrease in order. If monotonic is used to refer to sets, it means that each set contains the preceding set.

If an apportionment method satisfies house monotonicity, then it is free of the Alabama paradox. As the size of the house increases, each apportionment contains the preceding apportionments.

If an apportionment satisfies quota monotonicity, then whenever a state's quota increases or decreases, its apportionment will increase or decrease in the same way.

JOSEPH A. HILL'S METHOD FOR APPORTIONMENT

From 1850 to 1900, the population of the United States grew dramatically from 23 million to 75 million, an increase of more than 200%! Fourteen new states were added, and population shifted from the east to the west and from the country to the cities. In response to the growth in population, the size of the House of Representatives grew from 234 to 386 members. During this period of growth, several events turned the discussion over apportionment into a hot debate.

Politicians discovered that Hamilton's method was subject to some of the paradoxes you explored in Activity 14. Although Hamilton's method, enacted in 1852 as Vinton's Act, was the law for apportionment, it wasn't always strictly followed. In the 1860s and 1870s, no real method was used. The results of Hamilton's method were changed to satisfy states who felt they didn't have enough representatives. In the 1860s, 233 seats were apportioned using Hamilton's method, but then eight more seats were arbitrarily allotted to northern states. Similarly, in the 1870s the first apportionment resulted in 283 seats. The House size of 283 was chosen because at that size Hamilton's and Webster's methods led to the same apportionment. But several months later, nine additional seats were allotted. The new apportionment of 292 seats agreed with neither Hamilton's nor Webster's method.

Other things indicated that all was not well with apportionment. In the 1876 presidential election, Samuel J. Tilden received 4,300,590 popular votes to Rutherford B. Hayes's 4,036,298 votes. But the electoral college, which is influenced by the apportionment of the House, elected Hayes.

When the results of the 1880 census were reported to the House, the apportionment debates became more intense. It had become clear that Hamilton's method was plagued by paradox. Walter F. Willcox, a young professor in the philosophy department at Cornell, studied examples as well as congressional debates and concluded that Webster's method was the correct approach to apportionment. As a result, Webster's method was used in 1910 to apportion a House with 433 seats, together with a provision that the territories of Arizona and New Mexico receive one seat each should they be admitted as states before the next census. The number 433 was chosen because it was the lowest number that prevented any state from losing a seat.

In the meantime, a new method had been proposed, and the debate continued. Joseph A. Hill, chief statistician of the Division of Revision and Results, Bureau of the Census, argued that what we should care about in creating apportionment in the House is whether any state is better represented than any other state. By this he meant that the ratio of the population per representative should be almost the same for each state. He thought that the way to tell whether this was achieved was to consider how many times greater one ratio is than another and measure the difference on a percentage basis.

Hill's method for apportionment works this way:

Choose the size of the House to be apportioned. Give to each state a number of seats so that no transfer of any one seat can reduce the percentage difference in representation between those states.

This method doesn't yield a recipe for apportionment, but by using mathematics Edward V. Huntington created a method for apportioning the House following Hill's principle.

Hill's method works in a way similar to the other divisor methods. Like the other divisor methods, you need to find a divisor that will provide you with the desired House size. The difference is that, instead of using a rounding rule, you compare the quotient, q_i, obtained by dividing a state's population, p_i, by the divisor, d, to the geometric mean of $\left[\frac{q_i}{d}\right]$ and $\left[\frac{q_i}{d}\right] + 1$. (The brackets indicate the greatest integer function.) For example, if q_i is 15.542, look at $\sqrt{15 \cdot 16}$, which is approximately 15.492. Since 15.542 > 15.492 (the geometric mean), the state is allotted 16 representatives.

Consider This . . .

1. You can use Hill's method to apportion the Dale County student council with 26 members. First, you need to divide each school's population by the chosen divisor. Then compare this quotient to the geometric mean of $\left[\frac{q_i}{d}\right]$ and $\left[\frac{q_i}{d}\right] + 1$. If the quotient is greater than the geometric mean, then assign $\left[\frac{q_i}{d}\right] + 1$ representatives to the school. Otherwise, the school receives $\left[\frac{q_i}{d}\right]$ representatives. Use a divisor of 960 to compute the quotients in the table below and complete the apportionment of the 26-seat Dale County student council using Hill's method.

School	Student population	Quotient ($d = 960$)	Geometric mean	Number of representatives
North High	9061	9.439	$\sqrt{9 \cdot 10} = 9.487$	9
South High	7179			
Valley High	5259			
Meadow High	3319			
Ridge High	1182			
Total	26,000			

2. Compare the results of your student council apportionment using Hill's method to the results obtained using other apportionment methods. Which method seems fairest and why?

School	Hamilton's method	Jefferson's method	Webster's method	Adams's method
North High	9	10	9	9
South High	7	7	8	7
Valley High	5	5	5	5
Meadow High	4	3	3	3
Ridge High	1	1	1	2

Explore Further

3. Mountain County is forming an all-county handball team to participate in the upcoming national tournament. The handball committee has decided to apportion athletes to the all-county handball team from each handball association in the county using Hill's method. Complete the table to determine the apportionment for an all-county handball team with 13 players.

Club	Number of players	Quotient ($d = 100$)	Geometric mean	Number of athletes	Ideal quota
Rainier	501				
Adams	332				
Whitney	53				
St. Helens	46				
Hood	15				
Shasta	58				
Total	1005				

4. Does the apportionment of the handball players satisfy quota? What do you notice about the distribution of players in the various counties that might account for this result?

5. Use Hill's method to apportion SuperTec's board for a board of trustees with six members.

Department	Number of employees	Quotient ($d = 265$)	Geometric mean	Number of representatives
Development	241			
Production	673			
Sales	368			
Service	173			
Total	1455			

6. Are you satisfied with the results of the apportionment of SuperTec's Board? Why or why not?

7. Compare the results of the SuperTec apportionment using Hill's method to the results using the methods shown in the table below. Which method would you recommend?

Department	Hamilton's method	Jefferson's method	Webster's method	Adams's method
Development	2	1	1	1
Production	2	3	3	2
Sales	1	1	1	2
Service	1	1	1	1

Calculator Exploration

8. A programmable calculator or a computer spreadsheet program can greatly simplify the calculations for Hill's method. Develop a calculator routine for Hill's method and describe it, or use the program your teacher provides.

9. Use a calculator program or a computer spreadsheet program to find out how many seats have to be added to the student council before Ridge High receives a second seat.

10. Use a calculator program or a computer spreadsheet program to apportion 23 members to the Broad County hospital board using Hill's method and Webster's method.

Hospital	Number of patient beds	Hill apportionment	Webster apportionment
Grand Hospital	1518		
Mercy Hospital	1305		
Sunshine Hospital	865		
Rose Hospital	499		
Brookfield Hospital	296		
Littlefield Hospital	210		
Total			

How do the results using Hill's method compare to the results using Webster's method? Which method do you think is fairer?

Research

11. Do some research and find out how the geometric mean between two numbers can be represented geometrically.

12. Experiment with pairs of consecutive positive integers and make some conjectures relating the arithmetic mean and geometric mean of the two numbers. Show that your conjectures are true using geometry.

13. What is the current status of the apportionment debate? You can find interesting information about voting and apportionment on the Internet as well as at your local library. It might also be helpful to write to your representative in the House.

TEACHER'S NOTES

This activity introduces the method that is used today to apportion the House of Representatives. It was first described by Joseph A. Hill and was further developed by Edward V. Huntington. This method is also known as the method of **equal proportions**. Congress adopted this method in 1940 and has used it ever since.

Surprisingly, this method does not satisfy quota. This problem has not caused much controversy yet, because each of the four times that the equal proportions method has been used the specific apportionment obtained has, by chance, satisfied quota. There is no guarantee that this will continue to happen in the future. When the method gives an apportionment that doesn't satisfy quota, the apportionment debate may heat up again!

Be sure students understand how to compute the geometric mean and the arithmetic mean.

A calculator program for Hill's method follows Activity 18.

Consider This . . .

1.

School	Student population	Quotient ($d = 960$)	Geometric mean	Number of representatives
North High	9061	9.439	$\sqrt{9 \cdot 10} = 9.487$	9
South High	7179	7.478	$\sqrt{7 \cdot 8} = 7.483$	7
Valley High	5259	5.478	$\sqrt{5 \cdot 6} = 5.477$	6
Meadow High	3319	3.457	$\sqrt{3 \cdot 4} = 3.464$	3
Ridge High	1182	1.231	$\sqrt{1 \cdot 2} = 1.414$	1
Total	26,000			26

2. Answers will vary.

Explore Further

3.

Club	Number of players	Quotient ($d = 100$)	Geometric mean	Number of athletes	Ideal quota
Rainier	501	5.274	$\sqrt{5 \cdot 6} = 5.477$	5	6.461
Adams	332	3.495	$\sqrt{3 \cdot 4} = 3.464$	4	4.295
Whitney	53	0.558	$\sqrt{0 \cdot 1} = 0*$	1	0.686
St. Helens	46	0.484	$\sqrt{0 \cdot 1} = 0*$	1	0.595
Hood	15	0.158	$\sqrt{0 \cdot 1} = 0*$	1	0.194
Shasta	58	0.611	$\sqrt{0 \cdot 1} = 0*$	1	0.750
Total	1005			13	

*A team with a quotient less than 1 automatically gets 1 representative.

4. The apportionment of handball players using Hill's method does not satisfy quota. When there are many small constituencies with a few large constituencies, quota will sometimes be violated since the smaller groups must be assigned at least one member.

5.

Department	Number of employees	Quotient ($d = 265$)	Geometric mean	Number of representatives
Development	241	0.909	$\sqrt{0 \cdot 1} = 0$	1
Production	673	2.540	$\sqrt{2 \cdot 3} = 2,449$	3
Sales	368	1.389	$\sqrt{1 \cdot 2} = 1.414$	1
Service	173	0.653	$\sqrt{0 \cdot 1} = 0*$	1
Total	1455			6

6. Answers will vary.

7. In this case, Hill's method gives the same apportionment as Webster's and Jefferson's methods. Answers will vary.

Calculator Exploration

8. Answers will vary.

9. Six seats have to be added before Ridge High gets a second seat.

10.

Hospital	Number of patient beds	Hill apportionment ($d = 203$)	Webster apportionment ($d = 200$)
Grand Hospital	1518	7	8
Mercy Hospital	1305	6	7
Sunshine Hospital	865	4	4
Rose Hospital	499	3	2
Brookfield Hospital	296	2	1
Littlefield Hospital	210	1	1
Total	4693	23	23

In this particular case, Hill's method seems to favor the smaller hospitals. In general, in comparing Hill's method and Webster's method, the former will tend to favor the smaller units.

Research

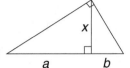

11. In the diagram at right, *x* is the geometric mean between *a* and *b*

12. The arithmetic mean is always greater than or equal to the geometric mean. In the diagram, the dashed line represents the length of the arithmetic mean. The radius of the circle is the arithmetic mean because the sum of a and b is the diameter. Dividing this sum by 2 gives you the radius. The altitude in the right triangle represents the geometric mean. The diagram shows that the geometric mean can be no longer than the radius of the circle.

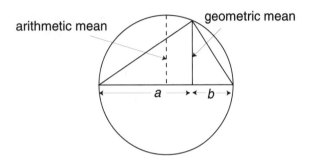

13. Help your students find the addresses of their representatives. These are often found in local phone books, and some local newspapers publish them on a regular basis. Many representatives also have an e-mail address that can be found by searching on the Internet using the keywords "House of Representatives." To find more information about the ongoing apportionment debate, students can search the Internet using keywords such as "apportionment" and "voting reform."

CHOOSING A METHOD: MATHEMATICS OR POLITICS?

Joseph Hill's method was championed by Edward V. Huntington, who was a classmate of Hill at Harvard University. Huntington was a professor of mechanics and mathematics at Harvard, and in 1921 he learned about Hill's method to find apportionments. He renamed Hill's method the **method of equal proportions** and from then on considered Hill's method to be his own invention.

Huntington argued strongly for the adoption of Hill's method, while Walter Willcox argued equally strongly for the adoption

The debate over Hill's and Webster's methods changed apportionment from a mathematical problem to a political struggle in Congress.

of Webster's method. A panel of four mathematicians was called in to review the problem, and to Huntington's delight they affirmed that Hill's method was the preferred method.

> The method of [Hill] is preferred by the committee because it satisfies the [relative difference] test . . . when applied either to sizes of congressional districts or to numbers of Representatives per person, and because it occupies mathematically a neutral position with respect to emphasis on larger and smaller States.[1]

Several factors led to the adoption of Hill's method. The House was never apportioned based on the 1920 census, because the new apportionment using Webster's method would have resulted in a huge loss of seats for rural areas. Congress was unable to agree on an apportionment and decided to disregard the 1920 census results, using the justification that during the war many people had temporarily left farms to seek work in cities and that, furthermore, rural areas had been grossly undercounted because the census had been taken in the middle of an unusually severe winter.

The failure to apportion Congress in the 1920s was in direct violation of the Constitution and created a great deal of uproar. People worried that, since the 1930 census would show an even greater loss of population in rural areas, reapportionment would be even more difficult. In response to this fear, Congress passed a bill in the summer of 1929 that required the president to send to Congress the representative populations of the states acquired from the census. Along with those populations, the president would send apportionments using three different methods: the method used after the previous census, the method of Webster, and the method of Hill. Once Congress received this information from the president, it would have a limited time period in which to reapportion itself. If it failed to do so, it would automatically be reapportioned using the method used after the previous census.

In 1930, the methods of Webster and Hill gave the same apportionment, leaving no grounds for argument. In 1940, the methods gave the same apportionment except for two states, Arkansas and Michigan.

State	Population	Hill apportionment	Webster apportionment	Quota
Arkansas	1,949,387	7	6	6.473
Michigan	1,949,387	17	18	17.453
U.S. total	131,006,184	435	435	435

The two apportionments changed the question of which method to use from a mathematical problem to a political problem. Arkansas was a safe Democratic state. Michigan tended to be Republican. A representative from Arkansas proposed an act for apportionment using Hill's method. When it came to a vote, every Democrat except those from Michigan voted for it. All the Republicans voted against it. The Senate held hearings and tried unsuccessfully to determine which method was unbiased. They recognized that every method of apportionment is arbitrary to some extent, and the decision became a partisan one. President Franklin D. Roosevelt signed Public Law 291 in November 1941, designating Hill's method for apportionment. Since then, it has been used to apportion every Congress.

Some political analysts believe that Webster's method is the fairest. There is no method that avoids the population paradox and always stays within quota. All the divisor methods avoid the Alabama paradox, and Webster's method is the divisor method that stays closest to quota. Statistically, under the present conditions in the United States, you can expect Webster's method to violate quota about 1 time out of every 1600 apportionments. That amounts to once every 16,000 years!

Hill's method violates quota more often than Webster's method, and it tends to favor small states. Webster's method seems to be more evenhanded in its treatment of large and small states.

Consider This . . .

1. What factors do you consider most important in deciding on an apportionment method?

2. Is there one apportionment method that is best in all circumstances?

3. Do you think a group like the U.S. House of Representatives can apportion itself fairly? Why or why not?

Research

4. Find out how large your county is, and design a countywide student council in which all the high schools are represented fairly. Decide how large the student council should be and what method should be used for apportionment. Using this method, apportion the student council and make a chart showing the apportionment along with the ideal quota for each school.

   After you have decided on the size and the method for creating the student council, decide how the representatives to the council are to be elected. Should each school have the same election process? What types of ballots will you use? How will you process the ballots to choose the schools' representatives? Should the methods used by the small and large schools be the same? What other questions will you want to answer in the process of choosing an election procedure?

   Prepare a presentation of your planned student council for your class. Include explanations of why you chose the methods you did.

TEACHER'S NOTES

The only permanent apportionment legislation is the act of 1929, which forces Congress to reapportion itself or be automatically reapportioned using the method that was used following the previous census. Arthur Vandenberg, the author of the act, explained in presenting it to the Senate:

> To identify any one method in this permanent act—whether the method of major fractions or equal proportions—would be to assume that science itself has traversed the subject with finality. Science is not thus static. . . . The last word by no means has been spoken. Scientists themselves will be among the first to recognize this fact, and, like the National Academy, scrupulously confess themselves limited to "the present state of knowledge." A permanent ministerial apportionment act should be susceptible of accommodation to the progressive state of knowledge.[2]

In the Consider This section, encourage students to voice their opinions about whether there is a "best" method. It may help them to consider which of the flaws in the methods is most disturbing and therefore to be avoided. Some students may be more disturbed by the violation of quota, and others by the paradoxes.

In his 1979 article, Jonathan Still suggests a moral to the question of the population paradox, which plagues many of the methods. He suggests that such paradoxes are curiosities and nothing more:

> The state populations are what they are; they define the apportionment problem which actually has to be solved. What the solution might be to another, hypothetical problem involving other, hypothetical populations is simply irrelevant. Changing the state populations changes the problem. In the final analysis, all of the various population paradoxes come down to nothing more than the observation that different apportionment problems will, in general, have different solutions. That is not particularly surprising.[3]

The above quote could lead to some interesting discussions with older students.

Answers

1–4. Answers will vary.

Reference Notes

1. G. A. Bliss, E. W. Brown, L. P. Eisenhart, and Raymond Pearl. "Report to the President of the National Academy of Sciences," February 9, 1929. In House, *Congressional Record*, 70th Congress, 2nd Session (1929), 70: 4966–4967. Also in House, Committee of the Census, *Apportionment of Representatives Hearings*, 76th Congress, 3rd Session (February 27, 28, 29 and March 1, 5, 1940).

2. Senate, *Congressional Record*, 71st Congress, 1st Session (1929), 71: 108. From speech of Arthur H. Vandenberg of Michigan, April 18, 1929.

3. Still (1979).

THE QUOTA METHOD FOR APPORTIONMENT

In the last few activities, you discovered that all of the apportionment methods that have been proposed for the House of Representatives are flawed. The divisor methods, such as the methods of Jefferson, Webster, Adams, and Hill, sometimes fail to satisfy quota. Hamilton's method, which is not a divisor method, does satisfy quota but is subject to several paradoxes. This leaves politicians in the position of needing to compromise and accept a less than perfect solution.

When people are stuck with a problem such as this, they

The quota method is the mathematical approach to apportionment.

often find it helpful to take a different approach. Michael L. Balinski and H. Peyton Young did just that when they devised an ingenious method called the Quota method for apportionment. Having proposed the method, they proved that

> the Quota method is the unique apportionment method that always satisfies quota and avoids the Alabama paradox.[1]

The Quota method works as follows. First choose the size of the House, s. Then start with a House with no seats and increase the size of the House by one seat at a time until it is full. Do this in rounds. In each round, the population of each state p_i is divided by its present number of seats plus one ($a_i + 1$). The additional seat is then assigned to an eligible state with the largest value of $\frac{p_i}{(a_i + 1)}$. (A state is eligible if giving it another seat would not lead to violating the upper quota with the new House size.)

The students of Broad County and Dale County decided to put their heads together and try the Quota method to apportion the Dale County student council.

The table below gives the student populations of the schools in Dale County.

School	Student population	Ideal quota
North High	9061	9.061
South High	7179	7.179
Valley High	5259	5.259
Meadow High	3319	3.319
Ridge High	1182	1.182
Total	26,000	26

In the first round, each school has no seats, so $(a_i + 1) = 1$ for all the schools. Therefore, in this round, $\frac{p_i}{(a_i + 1)} = p_i$ for each school, so North High, with the largest population, gets the first seat. This seat is entered in the table in the column labeled Round 1. In each round, check to see if the school with the largest value of $\frac{p_i}{(a_i + 1)}$ is eligible for a seat. To do this, compute the ideal quota of each school for that council size. This computation has been done for you and is summarized in the table below.

Upper Quota for Each School at House Sizes from 1 to 26.

School \ Round	1	2	3	4	5	6	7	8	9	10	11	12	13
North High	1	1	2	2	2	3	3	3	4	4	4	5	5
South High	1	1	1	2	2	2	2	3	3	3	4	4	4
Valley High	1	1	1	1	2	2	2	2	2	3	3	3	3
Meadow High	1	1	1	1	1	1	1	1	1	1	2	2	2
Ridge High	1	1	1	1	1	1	1	1	1	1	1	1	1

School \ Round	14	15	16	17	18	19	20	21	22	23	24	25	26
North High	5	6	6	6	7	7	7	8	8	9	9	9	10
South High	4	5	5	5	5	6	6	6	7	7	7	7	8
Valley High	3	4	4	4	4	4	5	5	5	5	5	6	6
Meadow High	2	2	3	3	3	3	3	3	3	3	4	4	4
Ridge High	1	1	1	1	1	1	1	1	2	2	2	2	2

In the first round, North High is eligible for a seat. In the second round, compute and compare $\frac{p_i}{(a_i + 1)}$ for each school, namely, $\frac{9061}{2}, \frac{7179}{1}, \frac{5259}{1}, \frac{3319}{1}$, and $\frac{1182}{1}$. In this round, South School has the largest value and is eligible, so it receives a seat. The table below shows the apportionment at the end of Round 2.

School / Round	1	2	3	4	5	6	7	8	9	10	11	12	13
North High	1	1											
South High	0	1											
Valley High	0	0											
Meadow High	0	0											
Ridge High	0	0											
Total seats	1	2											

School / Round	14	15	16	17	18	19	20	21	22	23	24	25	26
North High													
South High													
Valley High													
Meadow High													
Ridge High													
Total seats													

Consider This . . .

1. Use the Quota method to finish the apportionment for Dale County. Be sure to check the ideal quota at each level to see if a school is eligible to receive a seat. If a school isn't eligible, assign the seat to the eligible school with the next largest value of $\frac{p_i}{(a_i + 1)}$.

2. Does the Quota method seem fair? Why or why not?

3. How do the results of this method compare to the results of the other methods you have tried? Which method do you prefer?

School	Hamilton's method	Jefferson's method	Webster's method	Adams's method
North High	9	10	9	9
South High	7	7	8	7
Valley High	5	5	5	5
Meadow High	4	3	3	3
Ridge High	1	1	1	2

The Quota method was invented in an attempt to create an apportionment method that always satisfies quota and is free of paradoxes. Recall, that the divisor methods do not always satisfy quota and that Hamilton's method is not free from paradox. Another concern is bias. An apportionment method should not be biased toward either large or small states. Although Balinski and Young realized that it is impossible to satisfy all of these criteria, they believed it is more important to avoid paradoxes than to always satisfy quota.

Explore Further

4. Use the Quota method to apportion the Mountain County handball team with 13 players.

Handball Association	Votes	1	2	3	4	5	6	7	8	9	10	11	12	13
Rainier	501													
Adams	394													
Whitney	156													
St. Helens	149													
Total	1200													

5. Use the Quota method to reapportion the Mountain County handball team when six new players move in. What do you notice? Is this fair?

Handball Association	Votes	1	2	3	4	5	6	7	8	9	10	11	12	13
Rainier	501													
Adams	400													
Whitney	156													
St. Helens	149													
Total	1206													

6. Use the Quota method to apportion SuperTec's board for a board of trustees with six members.

Department	Number of employees	Apportionment
Development	241	
Production	673	
Sales	368	
Service	173	
Total	1455	

7. What problems did you find with the SuperTec apportionment? How can you modify the Quota method to fix these problems?

8. Compare the results of the SuperTec apportionment using the Quota method to the results using the methods shown in the table below. Which method would you recommend?

Department	Hamilton	Jefferson	Webster	Adams
Development	2	1	1	1
Production	2	3	3	2
Sales	1	1	1	2
Service	1	1	1	1

Calculator Exploration

Questions 9–11 refer to the apportionment of Dale County, which you explored above. Develop a calculator routine for the Quota method, or use the program provided by your teacher.

9. How many seats will each school get if the size of the student council in Dale County is increased to 27?

10. If only the size of the council is increased, at what size will Ridge High get an additional seat? Do you think this is fair?

11. Design a variation of the Quota method that will fix the problems you discovered in Question 7.

Reference Note

1. Balinski and Young (1975)

TEACHER'S NOTES

This activity introduces the Quota method, which at first glance appears to offer a solution to the problem of apportionment. However, when students investigate more closely in the Explore Further section of the activity, they discover that this method has problems of its own. It is subject to the population paradox, meaning that changes in population are not always reflected in the number of seats allocated.

This activity is more rewarding (and less frustrating) for students if they can use programmable calculators. Encourage your students to figure out a calculator routine for computing the apportionment that will aid them in record keeping as well. If they need suggestions, you can suggest the following routine.

Enter the populations of the schools, p_i, in list 1 and the number of seats each school has, a_i, in list 2. In list 3, enter the quotient $\frac{\text{list } 1}{\text{list } 2 + 1}$. This gives the value of $\frac{p_i}{(a_i + 1)}$. Students can compare the values in this list and decide which school receives the seat in the given round. They should record their results in their table and add 1 to the corresponding school in list 2. This process can be repeated until the council reaches the desired size. However, before giving another seat to any group, students need to check that the ideal quota for that size council will not be violated. A table of the ideal quotas for each council size is provided for the questions regarding Dale County. For the other questions, students may find it helpful to calculate the ideal quota for each school for each round in list 4.

A calculator program for the Quota method follows Activity 18.

Answers

Consider This . . .

1. Note that in going from a council size of 10 to 11, North High has the largest value of $\frac{p_i}{(a_i + 1)}$ but is not eligible to receive the seat, so South High receives the seat.

School \ Round	1	2	3	4	5	6	7	8	9	10	11	12	13
North High	1	1	1	2	2	2	3	3	3	4	4	5	5
South High	0	1	1	1	2	2	2	2	3	3	4	4	4
Valley High	0	0	1	1	1	1	1	2	2	2	2	2	3
Meadow High	0	0	0	0	0	1	1	1	1	1	1	1	1
Ridge High	0	0	0	0	0	0	0	0	0	0	0	0	0
Total seats	1	2	3	4	5	6	7	8	9	10	11	12	13

School \ Round	14	15	16	17	18	19	20	21	22	23	24	25	26
North High	5	6	6	6	7	7	7	8	8	8	8	9	10
South High	4	4	5	5	5	6	6	6	6	6	7	7	7
Valley High	3	3	3	4	4	4	4	4	4	5	5	5	5
Meadow High	2	2	2	2	2	2	2	2	3	3	3	3	3
Ridge High	0	0	0	0	0	0	1	1	1	1	1	1	1
Total seats	14	15	16	17	18	19	20	21	22	23	24	25	26

2. Answers will vary.

3. Answers will vary.

Explore Further

4.

Handball association	Votes	1	2	3	4	5	6	7	8	9	10	11	12	13
Rainier	501	1	1	2	2	3	3	3	3	4	5	5	5	6
Adams	394	0	1	1	2	2	2	2	3	3	3	4	5	5
Whitney	156	0	0	0	0	0	1	1	1	1	1	1	1	1
St. Helens	149	0	0	0	0	0	0	1	1	1	1	1	1	1
Total	1200	1	2	3	4	5	6	7	8	9	10	11	12	13

5. In going from a team size of 11 to 12 players, the Rainier handball association has the largest value but isn't eligible. The Adams handball association isn't eligible either, so the Whitney handball association gets a second player.

Handball association	Votes	1	2	3	4	5	6	7	8	9	10	11	12	13
Rainier	501	1	1	2	2	3	3	3	3	4	5	5	5	6
Adams	400	0	1	1	2	2	2	2	3	3	3	4	4	4
Whitney	156	0	0	0	0	0	1	1	1	1	1	1	2	2
St. Helens	149	0	0	0	0	0	0	1	1	1	1	1	1	1
Total	1206	1	2	3	4	5	6	7	8	9	10	11	12	13

This example demonstrates the population paradox. Even though the Adams handball association gained players relative to all the other clubs (its vote percentage increased from 32.8% to 33.2%), it lost a seat to the Whitney handball association!

6.

Department	Number of employees	Apportionment
Development	241	1
Production	673	3
Sales	368	2
Service	173	0
Total	1455	6

7. Answers will vary. Some students may think it is unfair that the service department is not represented on the board.

8. Answers will vary.

Calculator Exploration

9. South High will gain a seat; no other school is affected.

10. Ridge High will get an additional seat when the council contains 42 seats. The apportionment will be 15, 12, 8, 5, 2. The Quota method, like Jefferson's method, seems to favor the larger associations.

11. Answers will vary. Students may propose several variations of the Quota method. If they are stuck, you might suggest other tests to see which school should receive a seat in each round.

    One variation that still meets the criterion of quota and avoids the Alabama paradox is to assign the seat in each round to the school with the greatest difference between the ideal quota, q_i, in that round and the present number of seats, a_i. To use this variation, you would evaluate $q_i - a_i$ in each round.

Another variation is to determine the largest divisor d so that for all eligible parties $\sum \text{INT}\left[\frac{x_i}{d} + 0.5\right] = 1$ In other words, the additional seat at each level would be allocated to that eligible party whose number of votes x_i divided by d results in a decimal of 0.5 or larger. This variation is known as the Quota-Webster method.

PROPORTIONAL REPRESENTATION

The United States has a federal system in which geographical units are represented by single-member constituencies. This system developed in response to fairly homogeneous regions. However, over time these regions have become progressively less homogeneous, which may raise questions regarding the methods by which they are represented.

Many countries in the world use a proportional representation system.

Many nations use proportional representation (PR) systems of government, in which citizens are represented by political parties rather than by geographical regions. These systems developed because federal single-member systems make it difficult or impossible for small parties to be represented.

A country's proportional representation system is called **pure** if each voter casts a single vote for a party or party list and the representatives are then apportioned by the party itself. Only a few countries practice pure proportional representation. The Israeli Knesset and the Netherlands' Second Chamber are both pure proportional representation bodies.

Many countries use a proportional representation system in combination with other methods. A country might be divided into multimember electoral districts. In these countries, representatives are apportioned geographically; then, within the regions, proportional representation is used for apportionment. In other countries, pure proportional representation is used in one house of the representative branch. The different combinations of proportional representation and geographical representation lead to the use of different methods of apportionment.

The Israeli Knesset is elected through list proportional representation. The Knesset is a single chamber with 120 members. Every four years, when elections are held, each party presents the voters with its platform and a list of its candidates for the Knesset. Each party lists the candidates in order of importance by their criteria, and each list can have up to 120 candidates. Each voter then votes for a party, not a candidate. Once the results of the election are known, seats are apportioned to each party using Jefferson's method, which is referred to in much of the world as d'Hondt's method. In this way, the country is represented as a single constituency with 120 representatives.

List proportional representation might work in a small town as follows. The town of Midlands needs to elect two representatives to its countywide residents' association. Two opposing parties have emerged: the Conservative Party and the Liberal Party. The major issue in town politics is change. The Conservative Party members want change to occur very slowly, if at all. The Liberal Party members want a number of changes to happen quickly. They want to improve the city's water supply and add speed bumps to some roadways, and the most radical members of the party want to construct a central heating system for the town that would supply heat to all the homes.

There are 23 voters in the Midlands residents' association, 13 Conservatives and 10 Liberals. The Conservative candidates are Winston and Nadia, with Winston the more conservative of the two. The Liberal candidates are Theo and Rudy, with Rudy the more radical of the two. In a vote for the countywide residents' association, using ordinal ballots, the following preference schedules emerged:

Conservative		Liberal	
7	6	6	4
Winston	Nadia	Theo	Rudy
Nadia	Winston	Rudy	Theo
Theo	Theo	Nadia	Nadia
Rudy	Rudy	Winston	Winston

If two candidates were elected using Borda's method, Winston and Nadia would be declared the winners. In this case, the ten liberal voters would not be represented at all, even though they represent 43% of the residents' association.

To use list proportional representation, each residents' association member would vote for a party. If each member voted for the party he or she belonged to, the Conservatives would receive $\frac{13}{23}$ = 56.5% of the vote and would be entitled to that percentage of the available seats, namely, 1.13 seats. Similarly, the Liberals would draw $\frac{10}{23}$ = 43.5% of the vote and would be entitled to 0.87 seat. The residents' association would have to agree on an apportionment method, but it seems reasonable in this case that each party would receive one seat.

The problem that might occur with list proportional representation is that the voters' preference schedules are completely ignored. Which candidate fills the seat is up to the party. The parties could choose to be represented by their most radical candidates, namely, Winston and Rudy. This could increase polarization and lead to conflict. In any case, it would not be a good representation of the wishes of the society or the constituency as a whole, since all the Conservatives ranked Rudy last and all the Liberals ranked Winston last. Another problem with using list proportional representation is that appointed candidates are directly accountable not to the electorate but only to their respective parties. This could encourage blind allegiance and conformity to the party ideology in order to secure an electable place on the party list.

Consider This . . .

The Friends of the Arts of Broad County elect an Arts Commission, consisting of 18 people, once every three years. The members of the Arts Commission are actively involved in allotting money that the group raises for scholarships for young artists and for art classes that are made available to the public in Broad County. Over the past few years, the Friends of the Arts have split into four very distinct groups along the lines of the type of art they prefer most. The groups that have developed are the dancers, the musicians, the painters, and the sculptors. In the last election, the Friends of the Arts decided to use proportional representation to select their commission. The results of the vote are displayed in the following table.

Party	Number of votes
Dancers	164
Musicians	278
Painters	172
Sculptors	81

1. In your group, decide on a method and apportion the Arts Commission.

2. Why did you choose the method you used? Is there a particular benefit to one party in choosing a specific method?

3. If the painters and sculptors joined together as one group, would they benefit in the number of votes that they would receive? Investigate.

4. Compare and discuss the different methods your classmates suggested. What advantages did the various methods offer?

Explore Further

5. The citizens of Metropolis hold an election every four years to choose a five-member city judicial board. The citizens fall into three parties: Democrats, Republicans, and Independents. Use Hamilton's method to apportion the results of this year's election and the last election. Compare the results of the apportionments to the ideal quotas. What do you notice?

Party	Votes in last election	Ideal quota	Apportionment
Democrats	43,500		
Republicans	69,000		
Independents	37,500		

Party	Votes in this year's election	Ideal quota	Apportionment
Democrats	45,000		
Republicans	59,000		
Independents	46,000		

6. One of the issues that arises in proportional representation systems is the question of how large a party must be in order to obtain at least one seat. For the U.S. House of Representatives, this problem is solved in the Constitution, but the solution is not as clear-cut in countries using proportional representation. In Metropolis, the Socialist Party has been gaining members. How large do you think the party should be before it is represented on the five-member judicial board? Describe how you would make this decision.

7. A major difference between proportional representation and federal systems is that in federal systems the number of states remains fairly stable, while in some countries that use proportional representation the number of parties is constantly subject to change. Some parties fade away, while new ones form. Too much change in the number and composition of parties can lead to political instability. Which method of apportionment do you think would best encourage party stability?

Research

8. Some political activists believe that the time has come to reform the American political system. Investigate proportional representation in the United States. Under what circumstances could it be used in the United States? Who advocates it? Who opposes it? What would be some of the advantages and disadvantages of using a proportional representation system?

TEACHER'S NOTES

Proportional representation is particularly well suited for politically heterogeneous societies. A federal system, in which the winner takes all in each constituency, makes it very difficult for smaller parties to be represented.

There is, in fact, an election reform movement in the United States that advocates the adoption of proportional representation, at least at the local and state levels. Bob Richie, National Director of the Center for Voting and Democracy, suggests that many Americans do not vote because they do not feel represented. He points out that in the 1994 elections to the House of Representatives barely 22% of eligible voters helped elect candidates. In contrast, 75% of Germany's eligible voters helped elect candidates using a proportional representation system in their 1994 elections. Bob Richie states:

> Spreading political power, providing voters with more choices and allowing more segments of society to earn a place at the table of policy-making are all-important steps to providing greater long-term stability for our democracy.[1]

The Center for Voting and Democracy can be found on the World Wide Web. The Center's mailing address is 6905 Fifth Street NW, Suite 200, Washington DC 20012.

Your students may enjoy discussing the possibility of voting reform in the United States. Do they feel represented? Do they think they would feel better represented in a proportional representation system? Would they be more likely to vote?

Answers

Consider This . . .

1–4. Answers will vary.

Explore Further

5.

Party	Votes in last election	Ideal quota	Apportionment
Democrats	43,500	1.45	2
Republicans	69,000	2.3	2
Independents	37,500	1.25	1

Party	Votes in this year's election	Ideal quota	Apportionment
Democrats	45,000	1.5	1
Republicans	59,000	1.97	2
Independents	46,000	1.53	2

The Democrats received more votes but lost a seat. The Republicans received fewer votes but gained a seat.

6. Answers will vary.

7. Answers will vary. Jefferson's method favors larger states and therefore larger parties. It can be shown that it will therefore encourage coalitions of parties, and, in fact, it is the only method that encourages coalitions and avoids the population paradox.

Research

8. There is information on proportional representation on the World Wide Web. It can be found by doing searches with key phrases and words such as "proportional representation," "election," "voting," "democracy," and "apportionment."

Reference Note

1. Center for Voting and Democracy

CALCULATOR PROGRAMS

The calculator programs listed below are for the TI-82 and TI-83 calculators. The programs for Hamilton's method and the quota method must be entered separately. The programs for the divisor methods (Jefferson, Webster, Adams, and Hill) can be entered separately, or you can enter the divisor program. This program will compute the apportionment for any of the divisor methods.

Hamilton's Method

Store the populations in L1 before running the program. The final apportionment numbers are stored in L2.

```
Prgm:HAMILTON
ClrList L2,L3,L4,L5
ClrHome
Input "NUMBER OF SEATS",A
Input "NUMBER OF STATES",B
For(X,1,B,1)
iPart (L1(X)/sum L1*A)→L3(X)
If iPart (L1(X)/sum L1*A)=0
1→L3(X)
fPart (L1(X)/sum L1*A)→L4(X)
If iPart (L1(X)/sum L1*A)=0
0→L4(X)
End
If sum L3=A
Goto 2
L4→L5
L3→L2
0→X
Lbl 3
X+1→X
max(L5)→M
If L5(X)=M
Then
L3(X)+1→L2(X)
0→L5(X)
0→X
Else
End
If sum L2=A
Goto 2
Goto 3
Lbl 2
ClrHome
Disp L2
```

Jefferson's Method

Store the population data in L1 before running the program. You can use guess-and-check to find a divisor that will give the correct apportionment. The final apportionment numbers will be stored in L2.

```
Prgm:JEFFERSN
ClrHome
ClrList L₂
sum L₁→T
Input "NUMBER OF STATES ",B
Lbl 1
Input "DIVISOR ",D
For(X,1,B,1)
int (L₁(X)/D)→L₂(X)
End
For(X,1,B,1)
If L₂(X)=0
1→L₂(X)
End
ClrHome
Disp "THE NUMBER OF"
Disp "SEATS IS ",sum L₂
Disp "PRESS ENTER TO"
Disp "CONTINUE"
Pause
Menu("ARE YOU FINISHED","YES",3,"NO",1)
Lbl 3
ClrHome
Disp "THE DIVISOR IS",D
Disp "LOOK AT THE"
Disp "LIST IN L₂"
```

Webster's Method

Store the population data in L1 before running the program. You can use guess-and-check to find a divisor that will give the correct apportionment. The final apportionment numbers will be stored in L2.

```
Prgm:WEBST2
ClrHome
ClrList L₂
sum L₁→T
Input "NUMBER OF STATES ",B
Lbl 1
Input "DIVISOR ",D
For(X,1,B,1)
int (L₁(X)/D+.5)→L₂(X)
End
For(X,1,B,1)
If L₂(X)=0
1→L₂(X)
End
ClrHome
Disp "THE NUMBER OF"
Disp "SEATS IS ",sum L₂
Disp "PRESS ENTER TO"
Disp "CONTINUE"
Pause
Menu("ARE YOU FINISHED","YES",3,"NO",1)
Lbl 3
ClrHome
Disp "THE DIVISOR IS",D
Disp "LOOK AT THE"
Disp "LIST IN L₂"
```

Adam's Method

Store the population data in L1 before running the program. You can use guess-and-check to find a divisor that will give the correct apportionment. The final apportionment numbers will be stored in L2.

```
Pr9m:ADAMS2
ClrHome
ClrList L₂
sum L₁→T
Input "NUMBER OF STATES ",B
Lbl 1
Input "DIVISOR ",D
For(X,1,B,1)
-int (-L₁(X)/D)→L₂(X)
End
For(X,1,B,1)
If L₂(X)=0
1→L₂(X)
End
ClrHome
Disp "THE NUMBER OF"
Disp "SEATS IS ",sum L₂
Disp "PRESS ENTER TO"
Disp "CONTINUE"
Pause
Menu("ARE YOU FINISHED","YES",3,"NO",1)
Lbl 3
ClrHome
Disp "THE DIVISOR IS",D
Disp "LOOK AT THE"
Disp "LIST IN L₂"
```

Hill's Method

Store the population data in L1 before running the program. You can use guess-and-check to find a divisor that will give the correct apportionment. The final apportionment numbers will be stored in L2.

```
Pr9m: HILL
ClrHome
ClrList L₂
sum L₁→T
Input "NUMBER OF STATES ",B
Lbl 1
Input "DIVISOR ",D
For(X,1,B,1)
If L₁(X)/D≥√(int (L₁(X)/D)*(int (L₁(X)/D)+1))
int (L₁(X)/D)+1→L₂(X)
If L₁(X)/D<√(int (L₁(X)/D)*(int (L₁(X)/D)+1))
int (L₁(X)/D)→L₂(X)
End
For(X,1,B,1)
If L₂(X)=0
1→L₂(X)
End
ClrHome
Disp "THE NUMBER OF"
Disp "SEATS IS ",sum L₂
Disp "PRESS ENTER TO"
Disp "CONTINUE"
Pause
Menu("ARE YOU FINISHED","YES",3,"NO",1)
Lbl 3
ClrHome
Disp "THE DIVISOR IS",D
Disp "LOOK AT THE"
Disp "LIST IN L₂"
```

Quota Method

This program will compute the apportionment using the Quota method. Store the populations in L1 before running the program. The final apportionment numbers will be stored in L2.

```
Pr9m:QUOTA
ClrHome
ClrList L2,L3
1→T
Input "HOW MANY SEATS",S
Input "HOW MANY STATES",N
For(X,1,N,1)
0→L2(X)
End
Lbl 1
For(X,1,N,1)
(L1(X)/(L2(X)+1)→L3(X)
End
For(X,1,N,1)
If L3(X)=max(L3) and L2(X)+1>-int -(L1(X)/sum L1*T)
0→L3(X)
If L3(X)=max(L3) and L2(X)+1≤-int -(L1(X)/sum L1*T)
L2(X)+1→L2(X)
End
If sum L2=S
Goto 2
T+1→T
Goto 1
Lbl 2
Disp L2
```

Divisor Methods

This program will compute the apportionments for all of the divisor methods. If you use this program, you will not need to use the programs listed above for Jefferson's, Webster's, Adam's, and Hill's methods. Store the population data in L1 before running the program. You can use guess-and-check to find a divisor that will give the correct apportionment. The final apportionment numbers will be stored in L2.

```
Menu("ARE YOU FINISHED","YES",3,"NO",1)
Pr9m:DIVISOR
ClrList L2
sum L1→T
Disp "WHICH METHOD"
Disp "1:JEFFERSON"
Disp "2:WEBSTER"
Disp "3:ADAMS"
Disp "4:HILL"
Input C
Input "NUMBER OF STATES ",B
Lbl A
Input "DIVISOR ",D
For(X,1,B,1)
If C=1
Goto 1
If C=2
Goto 2
If C=3
Goto 3
If C=4
Goto 4
Lbl E
End
For(X,1,B,1)
If L2(X)=0
1→L2(X)
End
ClrHome
Disp "THE NUMBER OF"
Disp "SEATS IS ",sum L2
Disp "PRESS ENTER TO"
Disp "CONTINUE"
Pause
Menu("ARE YOU FINISHED","YES",B,"NO",A)
Lbl 1
int (L1(X)/D)→L2(X)
Goto E
Lbl 2
int (L1(X)/D+.5)→L2(X)
Goto E
Lbl 3
⁻int (⁻L1(X)/D)→L2(X)
Goto E
Lbl 4
```

```
If L1(X)/D≥√(int (L1(X)/D)*(int
(L1(X)/D)+1))
int (L1(X)/D)+1→L2(X)
If L1(X)/D<√(int (L1(X)/D)*(int
(L1(X)/D)+1))
int (L1(X)/D)→L2(X)
Goto E
Lbl B
ClrHome
Disp "THE DIVISOR IS",D
Disp "LOOK AT THE"
Disp "LIST IN L2"
```

BIBLIOGRAPHY

Balinski, Michel L., and H. Peyton Young. *Fair Representation: Meeting the Ideal of One Man, One Vote*. West Hanover, Massachusetts: Halliday Lithograph, 1982.

Balinski, Michel L., and H. Peyton Young. "The Quota Method of Apportionment." *American Mathematical Monthly.* (Aug–Sept 1975) 82, 701–730.

Brams, Steven J., and Peter C. Fishburn. *Approval Voting*. Boston: Birkhäuser, 1983.

Brams, Steven J., and Peter C. Fishburn. "Alternative Voting Systems." *Political Parties and Elections in the United States: An Encyclopedia*, Vol I. L. Sandy Maisel (ed.) New York: Garland, 1991.

de Villiers, Michael. *The Mathematics of Voting: Is Democracy Mathematically Obtainable?* Durban, South Africa: CASME, 1994.

Fishburn, Peter C., and Steven J. Brams. "Paradoxes of Preferential Voting." *Mathematics Magazine* 56(4) (1983) 207–214.

Consortium for Mathematics and Its Applications. *For All Practical Purposes*. Lynn A. Steen (ed.) New York: W. H. Freeman and Company, 1988.

Hoffman, Paul. *Archimedes' Revenge*. New York: W.W. Norton & Company, 1988.

Malkevitch, Joseph. *The Mathematical Theory of Elections*. HiMap Module 1. Arlington, Massachusetts: COMAP, 1989.

Still, Jonathan W. "A Class of New Methods for Congressional Apportionment." *SIAM J. APPL Math* 37(2) (Oct 1979) 401–418.

Center for Voting and Democracy. Available HTTP: http://www.igc.apc.org/cvd/

ABOUT THE AUTHORS

Leslie Johnson Nielsen

Leslie Johnson Nielsen graduated from Swarthmore College with a B.A. in mathematics and psychology, and she received her M.S. in mathematics education from California State University. She has taught in Pennsylvania, California, and Denmark.

Leslie is now a teacher and a freelance editor working and communicating electronically from her present home in Denmark. *Is Democracy Fair?* is her first book.

Michael de Villiers

Michael de Villiers graduated from the University of Stellenbosch, South Africa. After teaching mathematics and science in Karasburg, Namibia, and Diamantveld, Kimberley, he worked at the Research Unit for Mathematics Education at the University of Stellenbosch. During this time he completed a B.Ed., a M.Ed., and a D.Ed., and he spent a year on sabbatical at Cornell University on Rotary Foundation and Harry Crossley scholarships.

Since 1991 Michael has taught both undergraduate and graduate courses in mathematics education at the University of Durban-Westville, South Africa. He has published six books and over 90 articles, many of which have appeared in international journals. Since 1988 he has been the editor of Pythagoras, the official journal of the Association for Mathematics Education of South Africa. He is a regular speaker at local and international conferences on mathematics and mathematics education. He is also a member of several international organizations, including the PME Working Group on Geometry, COMAP, MAA, and the AMS. His main research interests are geometry, applications and modeling, and the history and philosophy of mathematics.